Illustrated by El Davo

To Olive, you're my inspiration
To Wilbur, your energy is infectious
To Tammy, you ooze kindness
This book was written by all of us x

Todd has taught thousands of delegates around the world, and after completing the course, each one is asked, 'What will you do differently now?'

Here follows a selection of their responses, which all start with

"I will…"

'… achieve my goals whatever it may take.' [Charidimos V]
'… be much more confident.' [Hadra A]
'… be more confident talking to new people.' [Elizabeth G]
'… be more grateful about being myself.' [Mohamad A]
'… be a better version of myself.' [Nicole E]
'… believe in myself.' [Maddi M]
'… change.' [Alex M]
'… achieve my potential.' [Abdulla R]
'… be more productive.' [Fahmid C]
'… feel comfortable being myself to others.' [Elissar B]
'… be more resilient to the voices in my head.' [Natasha J]
'… be more aware of the potential that I have.' [Emine O]
'… start improving my habits and focus on priorities.' [Marta M]
'… be more interactive with others.' [Dongho L]
'… manage my problems well.' [Umar T]
'… be more open.' [Marta O]
'… handle setbacks better.' [Rosemary C]
'… stop coming up with excuses.' [Javor G]
'… be more positive.' [Mathilda C]
'… be more motivated to achieve my goals.' [Iva K]
'… strive to better my self-discipline.' [Sean M]
'… step out of my comfort zone.' [Margherita C]
'… be more organized.' [Abdul R]
'… have more purpose in everything I do.' [Luksa K]

'… be more committed towards my goals.' [Mohamed A]

'… be more productive.' [Sharon S]

'… face my fears.' [Tanu C]

'… be more confident in myself.' [Madalina M]

'… have purpose in my actions.' [Louise M]

'… face the tasks that I avoid because of fear.' [James W]

'… step out of my comfort zone.' [Daniela B]

'… start changing unhealthy habits.' [Augustin L]

'… set goals for myself.' [Nilay S]

'… pursue my goals.' [Jeremiah U]

'… implement mindfulness.' [Lauren C]

'… be an active listener.' [Anira B]

'… set my goals.' [Imani S]

'… know myself better.' [Abhishek B]

'… not be afraid to share my thoughts with others.' [Disha S]

'… make the most of what I have.' [Tiffany D]

'… be more authentic.' [Ellarene C]

'… accept myself.' [Alice V]

'… apply for jobs I was unsure about.' [Marco A]

'… believe in my ability.' [Hannah S]

'… be more confident in myself.' [Amy F]

'… appreciate different opinions.' [Ana M]

'… work harder towards my goals.' [Andres G]

'… face my future strong.' [Arjunan R]

'… commit with purpose.' [Camilo R]

'… push myself to leave my comfort zone.' [Daniel C]

'… keep improving myself.' [Emmanuel O]

'… control my inner voice.' [Hiren T]

'… be a better leader.' [Ieva G]

'... adopt mindfulness and talk to strangers.' [James T]

'... feel more confident around people.' [Jessica F]

'... be more self-aware.' [Kabilas P]

'... feel more confident to apply for certain jobs.' [Katherine H]

'... put myself in the shoes of others more often.' [Kilian B]

'... take responsibility for my life.' [Lanja R]

'... take risks.' [Lauren M]

'... get out of my comfort zone.' [Madhumitha K]

'... listen more.' [Michal C]

'... be more confident.' [Nantia B]

'... have more confidence in myself.' [Polly S]

'... be more mindful.' [Rosie G]

'... be more ready to take the lead.' [Samuel S]

'... be more introspective.' [Sian W]

'... take better care of my health.' [Sushma S]

'... always say positive things about myself.' [Toyyibat B]

'... be more resilient.' [Yakubu S]

'... be willing to step out of my comfort zone.' [Sabrina C]

'... continue to be me.' [Samantha C]

'... make a difference.' [Debbie F]

'... believe in myself more.' [Manvinder D]

'... express myself better.' [Hasit G]

'... be kinder to myself.' [Jad J]

'... trust other people more.' [Ashley A]

'... stop trying to solve other people's problems.' [Brandon M]

'... be more understanding.' [Noi B]

By the end of this book, what will you be doing?

TABLE OF CONTENTS

INTRODUCTION

You have lived on this planet for quite some time now. How's it going?

No really. I'm interested. Or rather, you are. So, pause, just for a few seconds to really ponder the question: How is life turning out for me?

Perhaps you're thinking, 'It's a huge freakin' mess, and I don't know how to dig myself out.' Or maybe, 'Things are actually going pretty well, but is this it?' No matter how you respond to this question, if you want to get the most out of life, then this book will help you discover the authentic human you are and lay the foundations for living the life you are truly capable of living.

To truly Own Life takes some time, so be patient with the book and yourself. Give the concepts space to breathe, and your experiments the necessary time to achieve your desired results. Throughout this book, you'll be learning how to live with greater self-confidence and set your path to own your future.

Unlike many self-help books, we are not attempting to turn you into someone new, to add another mask, which is exhausting to live up to. You will always be you, and we want you to be ALL of you, ALL of the time.

To the outside world, you may look like a regular student or worker, and this may be the person that you perceive yourself to be day-by-day. However, when you remove the external image, peel back the layers to find the authentic you, that's when the magic begins to happen. You'll start to notice the layers that have built up, which can fog your ability to shine as a wonderfully unique, contentedly idiosyncratic human being.

When you allow yourself, being you is so easy, and nobody else does it better!

Before we start, it's helpful to get a baseline on how things are really going for you. Answer these questions honestly based on your experience of the last six months. Rate your answers to the following statements using this scale:

strongly disagree	disagree	neutral	agree	strongly agree

- I know and accept myself for who I am.
- I believe I can become good at anything I choose to put my mind to.
- I maintain a positive emotional state of mind regardless of what is going on around me.
- I push through fear to accomplish things that are uncomfortable.
- What I do is aligned to a deeply held sense of purpose.
- I make the most of life by using my time wisely.
- I am like a battery, always full of energy and ready to go.
- I enjoy trusting, respectful relationships with everyone in my life.

What if you could nudge your scores further to the right? It doesn't matter where you start, any nudge would be good!

And just imagine what life would be like if you could live it way over to the right-hand side most of the time. That's our goal together.

Your life is in your hands. How much you move depends on how much you invest in it. The questions you just answered put you on the path to becoming more self-aware, and it's through the lens of 'yourself' that we'll do great work together. Yes, there are models and theories, lots of them in fact, but it's how you relate to them that matters – so when there's a pause in the text and a question for you to ponder, really do it.

Throughout the book, you'll see sections titled 'Reflect & Write'. This is your invitation to do just that. Take some quiet time to consider each of the questions, allow your thoughts and feelings to emerge, and then crystalize them by putting pen to paper. The act of writing down your thoughts helps them to settle in your mind and brings a comforting level of clarity. I don't think of you as readers, I think of you as participants, so read this book with a pen in your hand and your favourite notebook to fill.

The insights that you gain about yourself can be revelatory yet remain merely interesting. To shift the dial of your life requires action, and throughout the book you will be invited to conduct small experiments to tweak your ingrained behaviours.

From time-to-time you may have a question that you need some help with; or would like to connect with others who are struggling with similar issues; or would like to share a moment of enlightenment, or a piece of advice; or be inspired by other people's Own Life journey; or find out about free webinars on each chapter. For any of this, head over to www.ownlife.me and let's Own Life together.

Are you ready to live a more rewarding life? Sure, you are. Let's jump into the first chapter.

CHAPTER 1
WHO AM I?

Who am I, and why am I here? These are two significant questions with which to begin a self-development journey. Since the answers are constantly evolving, you may never find THE answer to either. However, not to contemplate these fundamental questions is to hand over the steering wheel of life to others.

By the end of this chapter, you will have a strong sense of your own identity and be completely OK with who you are right now. We will do this by exploring how your upbringing has shaped your character. What sets you apart from everyone else – how are you unique? What do you have to offer the world, and what would you like your contribution to be?

SOCIAL CONDITIONING
Programming Children

The environment into which each of us is born is unique – different to everyone else on the planet through its climate, history, culture, family shape, or sibling sequence. As babies, if our clan rejects us, we die, and therefore we are hard-wired with a longing for acceptance. To do this, we mimic others – taking particular notice of the behaviours of the grown-ups around us and conforming to fit in.

Even before we can talk, we begin to believe and value the same things as our society. These beliefs and values go in 'unfiltered', we're not judging at this age, we're absorbing. Children are likely to have the same beliefs about religion as their parents and in future, vote the same way. We learn what our parents determine to be useful or interesting, so our early skillset is programmed by the people around us.

All this comes together to shape our sense of identity; the things we say about ourselves (to ourselves). It's a list of 'I am's'. This whole process, whereby the significant people around us shape who we are, is termed 'social conditioning'.

You will see a little later how significant your specific social conditioning is on your daily habits, and to what extent you've already broken away from the conditioning of your early years. Consciously choosing your own path is known as 'self-determination' and could also be the subtitle of this book.

How Your Brain Is Wired

Compared to every other species, human brains are born 'underdeveloped'. But it is this unfinished nature of the brain that is also our most significant strength – because it makes us adaptable. The human brain is shaped by the details of life experiences, so it's 'livewired' rather than 'hardwired'.[1]

It's not the number of brain cells that change (children and adults have the same amount), it's the way they're connected. Over the first two years of life, as we experience sensory information, the neurons become rapidly connected until we have over 100 trillion synapses. From this moment onwards, the unused connections are pared back until only half remain, while those we use most become stronger.

Imagine rain falling on a hillside. Individual drops evaporate and leave no trace, while others fall together, forming rivulets, and eventually have the power to cut deeply into the landscape. Every hill is unique, and every shower is different. So too is the physical structure of your brain, every single life experience has shaped its microscopic details. The way your brain is wired is shaped by your past and is therefore different to everyone else's on the planet.

Your Social Conditioning

If you were writing your autobiography and the first chapter was titled 'Age 0 to 13', what would you write about? You might include your environment (including the people), the behaviours you were taught (deliberately and by observation), which skills were nurtured and the set of beliefs you adopted.

Reflect & Write: Write a few paragraphs to describe your life from birth to 13 years old. Next, recall what it was like to be 13 years of age. Stand in your school shoes as though you have time travelled into the past and write a list of at least 10 'I am... statements. For example, *I am shy, I am easy-going* and so on.

Your upbringing has shaped you. So what shape are you now? In the next section, we'll find out.

WHO ARE YOU TODAY?

What others see in you isn't you. It's a combination of what you're projecting (perhaps unconsciously), and what they notice (which depends on them, not you).

Reflect & Write: Consider five people from different parts of your life who know you really well. If you asked each of them in turn, and in strict confidence, to describe you in five words, what would they say? Stepping back and seeing all 25 words, what patterns or themes emerge?

What You Value

Our values considerably influence our behaviour, which in turn shape our destiny. Perhaps you've never considered what you value most and why – but you can deepen your self-awareness right now. From the list below, select the five values that you feel are most important to you (at this moment in your life):

- Accountability
- Achievement
- Balance
- Commitment
- Compassion
- Competence
- Cooperation
- Friendships
- Health
- Honesty
- Humour/fun
- Independence
- Integrity
- Initiative
- Intuition
- Leadership
- Making a difference
- Openness
- Personal growth
- Power
- Respect
- Responsibility
- Risk-taking
- Self-discipline
- Success
- Trust
- Teamwork
- Wisdom

Reflect & Write: Write a sentence or two about why you've chosen each value, and then score each one 0–10 based on how fully you have lived it over the past **two weeks** with 0 meaning not all and 10 meaning totally.

(Imagine you'd been followed around with a video camera every waking moment for the last couple of weeks and others get to rate your performance on YouTube. What would be your average score?) Did you rate yourself 10/10 for every one of them? Probably not. There's a range – some high, some low. Be OK with whatever the number is, this is self-awareness, not self-judgement.

Reflect & Write: Take one of the lower scores. Let's suspend judgement for a moment. If, with 'a click of the fingers' you are now living that value 10 out of 10 for the next month (without worrying about how this might happen), write down what is different for you, and what is different for others around you.

You've now contemplated a more satisfying future where you are fully living this value, and you know your present reality (your score from the past two weeks). It's time to begin the development journey with a single small step.

Reflect & Write: What can you do in the next 48 hours to begin to shift your current score upwards? You're not looking for a giant leap (although it's OK if that's what happens), you're merely attempting to become unstuck – to shift a habit and begin to move in the right direction. If you wish, you can now decide what to do with each of the other four values – what small step would you like to take to begin living each value more fully by the end of the week?

What You Believe

Take a look at the following belief statements. Which are true for you, or false, or perhaps neutral?

I believe that:

- My parents are rightly proud of me.
- Everything will turn out all right in the end.
- It's OK for the majority of my friends to be online.
- I'm not as nice as people think I am.
- The world is my oyster.
- Capitalism is a force for good.
- Quality of friendships is better then quantity.

We carry beliefs with us that have emerged from somewhere in our past and fundamentally shape our future. So, let's find out what some of yours are.

Reflect & Write: Set a timer on your phone for 90 seconds and complete this sentence as many times as you can in 90 seconds, 'I believe that...' Bring no judgement to what comes up, simply notice what thoughts arise and immediately write them down. The time pressure helps you to access your subconscious and to grow your awareness of your hidden drivers. There's plenty of time for editing later.

Now you've got some thoughts on the page, and the question about your personal beliefs logged in your subconscious, keep your notes with you, and add to the list when you think about it. See if it doubles over the next 10 days.

My Skillset

We all have a set of strengths that contribute to the positive state of our lives and a comparative set of weaknesses that may be more self-limiting. Let's start with the good stuff because we can probably find ways to do more of it, more often. Perhaps these are things we'll tell prospective employers; or just sit back for a few brief moments to feel good about ourselves.

Reflect & Write: Take each of these statements in turn, and jot down what comes up for you:

- *My most successful project was... And what I did particularly well was...*
- *When working in teams, I usually take the same role because...*
- *When facing challenges in my past, I overcome them by...*
- *The strengths that others acknowledge in me are...*

Reflect & Write: Now consider each of the five people who you selected earlier (see page 8), whom you know really well, what qualities do they have? Aim for a total of 20 or more positive attributes.

Was thinking about others easier or harder than thinking about your own strengths? Perhaps it felt less comfortable to consider your own qualities – and that may be because we can't see what we do well naturally, or because we've been socially conditioned not to boast and have zero practice at articulating what we're good at. We'll change that now. Look back through the notes that you've already taken.

Reflect & Write: What five things are you best at? Give each one a simple label and add an example of a situation that best paints a picture of you using this skill.

Now, let's consider the flipside of this coin, your weaknesses. By writing them down, their power to cause sleepless nights will dissipate, and by putting the impact into context, you can either let go of a problem that you thought you had, but don't, or make a decision to do something to reduce its impact.

> **Reflect & Write:** First, you may want to give this some context, such as at work, in teams, at home, when studying, etc. then list the top five weaknesses that hold you back from performing well. For each one, be specific about how it holds you back.

Reviewing your list, are there any weaknesses that have little bearing on your life outcomes? I can't speak a foreign language yet I work internationally. Is this fact having a significant impact on my life? If no, then I can simply accept that it's a skill I don't have and don't need, so I can let go of any concern about it.

What if the answer is 'yes and it has a significant impact'? Then accept that you *currently* don't have this skill. We tackle the desire to have it in Chapter 2.

My Recipe
Reviewing everything you've noted down so far, consider each section to be an ingredient in the person that is you: a jar of belief, a sprinkle of upbringing, a dash of strengths, a drop of weakness. You pour it all in, give it a stir and give it to a reporter to taste.

> **Reflect & Write:** What does the reporter write about you? Aim for about seven succinct statements that start *He/She is…*

Johari's Windows

Look at the list above and compare it to the one you made on page 8. There will be some differences in how you see yourself and how others see you. There's a model that can help us to frame the differences, (developed by psychologists Joseph Luft and Harrington Ingham in 1955 and endearingly known as 'Johari' by combining their first names).[2]

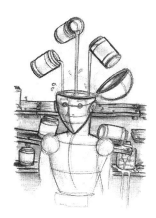

When we're being completely authentic, allowing others to see the true us, then we're operating in an open box – and there may be only a handful of people with whom we wear no mask. In the majority of our relationships, where trust isn't 100 per cent, we keep things private – work colleagues, flatmates, study partners only get to see the version of us that we want them to see.

Reflect & Write: What are you choosing to hide? And from whom? Make a list. When we get to the relationship section of this book, we'll return to these as they may be getting in the way of establishing trust.

Reflect & Write: Through the first chapter of this book, you've started to become aware of the things that you (deep down), already know about yourself. But we haven't done anything, yet, to make your blind spots visible. On page 8, you guessed what people may say about you. Now go and talk to those people and ask them a question: *If you had to describe me in five words, what would you say?*

ACCEPTANCE
The Myth of Okayness[3]

You may wish you were different – or perhaps that others saw you differently. This is very common. In fact, in the top 10 of 'How to...' Google searches in 2016 was 'How to accept myself for who I am.'

Sometimes we observe someone else and wish that we were more like them. But remember, you are only seeing what is open, what they are allowing you to see. There is a whole hidden side that they keep private. When you ask, 'How are you?' and they respond, just like you do, 'Fine thanks', or 'OK', this the 'Myth of Okayness'.

If you really ask, and they really trust you, then you realize everyone has insecurities about who they are, and a set of ways in which they would like to be different.

Consider people in the public eye who appeared to have everything and yet were or are fighting inner battles – Michael Jackson, Amy Winehouse, Princess Diana, George Michael, Tiger Woods, Marilyn Monroe. Who else

would you add to this list? There will be many famous and successful people whose struggles have not yet made it into public awareness.

If it's OK for someone else not to be perfect, then it's OK for you to be imperfect too. A perfect human doesn't exist, can't exist, and therefore it isn't you and never will be. I am not perfect and never will be, and neither will you. It's OK to be OK with not feeling OK about yourself, we all do in some way; it's what makes us human.

Denial Is Futile

All of your past experiences have led you to this moment, and while you may not consider yourself to be flourishing, they lay the roots for your growth. You are you. Your past is in the past. Therefore, you have no option but accept the embodiment of the you reading this sentence. You know what you've been through and how you have behaved; attempting to reject the past is futile. If you deny any thoughts or emotions, you'll be limiting your ability to grow and move beyond whatever is holding you back. Simply surrender to the peace that comes from acceptance. I am me, and for now, that is completely fine.

You Shape the You of the Future

While you can accept that you are an embodiment of your past experiences right now, it isn't a done deal that you will remain this way forever. By choosing your future experiences, you will be choosing to identify with new statements about yourself. As you'll see in the next chapter, you can choose to let go of whatever 'I AM' statements you're holding onto right now that are not serving you well. How you grow is dependent on how you decide to nourish your roots.

WHY AM I HERE?

The Keel of Your Boat[4]

Imagine a flat-bottomed sailing boat. When the wind blows, the boat moves with it – and when the wind direction changes, the boat does too. And when there's a gust, pop, it capsizes.

So boats have a keel that runs from front to back and cuts deep into the water. Now the boat moves in the direction it is pointing, (with the power of the wind captured by the sails), and stays upright while the storms blow strong.

A boat's keel is like your purpose in life. The more deeply connected you are with your sense of purpose, the more you're able to move in your chosen direction, achieving your dreams. The more deeply connected you are with your sense of purpose, the easier it is to stay upright when the winds of change blow and attempt to knock you off balance.

Does your life have a keel to keep you upright and pointing forwards? Is it there because of your social conditioning or because of your decisions?

Social Conditioned Purpose

We learnt earlier that social conditioning affects our sense of identity and shapes our purpose in life. From subtle unconscious bias related to the toys you were bought as a child, to 'help' from parents when choosing A-levels, and then degree courses; from social media influencers to the neighbours; what you are doing now has been influenced by the outside world.

When we're young, it's essential to listen to the advice of those people we trust to have our best interests at heart. At the right moments in life, it's important to recognize these influences AND ensure we are taking the ultimate decision about what we're choosing to do with our lives.

Reflect & Write: Consider what you are doing now. Who influenced 'your' decision, and how have they influenced it?

What Is My Purpose?

First, we're going to soften the feel, by substituting the word 'purpose' with the word 'intention', and simply look at what intentions you have for your future and why they are important. For example, what is your intention for this weekend? (i.e. what do you intend to do?) There may be several things, so just choose one that is likely to be your highlight.

This weekend I intend to hang out with my daughter doing something that we both enjoy. This is important to me because I feel as though, recently, we haven't spent quality time together, just the two of us. And that really matters to me because I want her to be able to talk to me openly as she enters her teenage years.

Reflect & Write: Now, over to you, complete this sentence: *This weekend I intend to... this is important to me because... and that REALLY matters to ME because...*

Notice what happened as you contemplated these three questions. You likely began with something that feels superficial – a decision to do something out of habit, or because of some logical reason. As you moved through to the final sentence, you may have found that it feels a little more profound – coming from your heart rather than your head. It's this last sentence that gives you an idea about why you are doing it. It is your purpose. And therefore, we can now enquire if there is a better way of achieving the same purpose this weekend.

When you wrote the second sentence, did you find yourself struggling to find something to write? Perhaps what you intend for this weekend isn't that important to you. Is there something else that you would rather be doing with the most precious commodity of all, time?

There are plenty of weekends in life, so the stakes aren't that high really – it was just a practice round. So, now let's expand the time horizon to six months.

Reflect & Write: What three intentions do you hold for yourself over the next six months? Follow the method from above, write down your intention, then why it is important to you, and finally, why that **really** matters.

Are you noticing a similar shift in your energy as you move through the series of questions? Allow the bottom sentences to be your keel.

Finally, we'll move the time horizon out to 10 years. This is sufficient time for you to be doing pretty much anything you could imagine. Just let the pen flow, knowing that whatever emerges right this minute, is simply what emerges this minute and can be edited, replaced, or enhanced at any moment in the future.

Reflect & Write: What three intentions do you hold for yourself? Complete the sentence: *In the next 10 years, I intend to...* And then follow the pattern from above: *This is important to me because...* And finally: *This REALLY matters to ME because...*

What you've written may have surprised you. Not many people spend focussed time considering the next 10 years of their life; and if it's the first time for you, then be OK with your first draft of your future. You'll refine it, tweak it, tear it up – whatever. It's good enough to have a glimpse, however fleeting, of the future version of you that sits within the version of you that exists today.

Bringing Intention to Life

It is possible to move through life without having a sense of purpose, and of course, it is possible to live a life without really having LIVED. By bringing intention to your future, you get connected to your keel. Here are some tips to help bring your intentions to life.

Tip 1: The Daily 3X

At the start of each day write down three things that will make this a great day (they have to be things within your control, so don't write something about the weather being nice!).

Tip 2: Annual Goals

What will make this a great year? Turn the intention into tangible milestones. If this year goes really well for you, what would you like to have achieved 365 days from now? Have a go now right now and then put monthly reminders in your calendar to check your progress.

Tip 3: Message in a Bottle

Have a guiding sentence that you can easily recall that helps you to make decisions. Will X or Y move me towards my life purpose? Know that this statement will evolve over time – but always have one.

Consider it this way: if you sat on a beach gazing out to sea and mulling over a significant life decision, what personalized message in a bottle would you like to wash up next to you which would help guide your decision?

Reflect & Write: What guiding message would you like to be reminded of every day? (Head to www.ownlife.me to be inspired by what others have written.)

Getting Aligned

Consider what you are doing now. I don't mean reading this book. I mean in your life. Is it aligned with your sense of purpose? If yes, then great.

If not, then great! Often we can't stop doing what we're doing immediately without there being short-term consequences. However, the long-term consequence of continuing to do something that isn't aligned with your sense of purpose is more catastrophic. So simply noticing there's a gap is great. Being able to articulate that gap with some precision is even better as it's the first step to closing it. And greatest of all – is to write it all down so you can refer to it as we progress through the book.

Reflect & Write: When comparing what you're doing in life now against your long-term intentions, write down what thoughts arise.

Concluding Thoughts

Using the exercises in this first chapter, you now have a deeper awareness of the imperfect, unique human being shaped by all the experiences of your past. We're also glimpsing what's even deeper inside – the core of your being, and what your purpose in life may be.

In Chapter 2, we turn the tables. Who you are is a product of where you've been (Chapter 1), but who you become is determined by where you go next, so let's start Owning Life.

CHAPTER 2
WHO I CAN BE

By accepting who you are today based on your past experience, you can now take active steps to decide who you'd like to be in the future. You are now an adult and the responsibility for who you are lies with you.

Since adolescence you have changed, you've overcome challenges, you've become good at some things, and with effort, you can become good at everything that you want to. In Chapter 2, we'll put a spotlight on your habits, improve willpower and demonstrate that it's effort rather than innate talent that holds the key to your future.

HOW HAVE YOU CHANGED?
Emerging from the Cocoon

You've seen how social conditioning affects who you are – and how things like beliefs and values are shaped by the people around you. However, we quite naturally begin the process of self-actualization – emerging from the childhood cocoon to become our unique

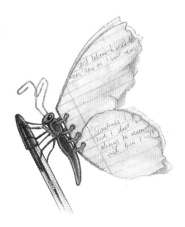

butterfly. During our teenage years, tensions between child and parent often come from the teenager spreading their wings, questioning some beliefs, and choosing their friends and their environment.

Reflect & Write: Reflecting on your teenage years, how did you emerge from the cocoon? Was it an easy transition, or were there tensions between you and your family? In what ways did you change? Write 10 changes that you are now noticing.

Reflect & Write: Looking back – what advice would you give to your 13-year-old self? Write a short paragraph.

Reflect & Write: How about the intervening years? In what ways have you changed since turning 20? Make a long list of skills, beliefs, environment, people you hang out with, what you do, what you wear, your hair, how you see yourself, and so on. Fill a page if you can.

When you look back, you'll notice that there have been significant changes – some of it was deliberate and planned, but much of it simply happened. There's a lot changing that you're not even aware of from moment to moment. Did you know, for example, that 98 per cent[5] of the atoms making up your body are replaced each year? Or when we say, 'it's in our blood', meaning something handed down through the generations, in fact, red blood cells only live for about four months?[6]

If you've ever believed that 'people can't change', it simply isn't true. You, me, and everyone else changes every day. Our daily experiences affect the synaptic connections in our brains. Change isn't only possible, it's inevitable.

Hermit crabs with too-small shells can't grow as fast as those with well-fitting shells and are likely to be eaten if they can't retract completely.

For us to Own Life, we must understand when we need to create more space to grow and be proactive about it rather than allowing the environment to squash us into an ill-fitting box.

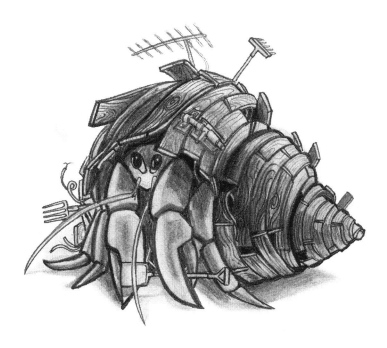

Back to the hermit crab for a moment – before moving into its new home, it must first choose to leave its snug environment, full of memories, and courageously scuttle into an expanse of no mans land where it is at its most vulnerable.

And so too, must we. The process of self-actualisation is not always comfortable, and at times, we have to summon real courage to leave our past behind.

SELF-ACTUALIZATION
Overcoming Challenges

Whomever you are today, whether you are intensely self-critical, or coolly self-confident, there is an even better version of you waiting to emerge from beneath the layers of social conditioning. It is possible to bring 'conscious' change at many levels: environmental, behavioural, capabilities, beliefs, values, or identity. It may seem hard now, but you've got some useful past experiences to draw from. It may seem daunting to leave the comfort of the past and take the first vulnerable 'crab-steps' into your future, so first let's look at how you've succeeded in getting to this moment in your life.

Reflect & Write: Consider the challenges from your past (e.g. moving schools, preparing for exams, delivering a speech, parents separating, finding a job, etc.), jot them down, aiming for 10 or more.

Focussing on the most difficult one, in the beginning, how were you feeling? Now you're reflecting on having successfully overcome it, how do you feel? How did you do it?

Now back to the other nine on your list. What strategies did you use to overcome those? Write down the strategies that you have successfully used in the past to overcome your challenges.

Life is full of challenges, and the ones in front of us seem more daunting than the ones behind us. Yet, once upon a time, those challenges too seemed insurmountable. But here you are, reflecting on the lessons they brought you. These enable you to face the future, and scuttle into the unknown.

Becoming More You

Throughout this book, you'll be identifying things that you want to shift to become an even better version of your true self. This process is termed 'self-actualization' and was first introduced by Adrian Maslow as the pinnacle of his 'Hierarchy of Needs'. Here is a selection of the most important characteristics, from his book *Motivation and Personality*.[7] Use the list to audit yourself – tick each statement that is true for you:

- Self-actualized people embrace the unknown and the ambiguous.
- They accept themselves, together with all their flaws.
- They prioritize and enjoy the journey, not just the destination.
- While they are inherently unconventional, they do not seek to shock or disturb.
- They are motivated by growth, not by the satisfaction of needs.
- Self-actualized people have a purpose.
- They are not troubled by the small things.
- Self-actualized people are grateful.
- They share deep relationships with a few but also feel identification and affection towards the entire human race.
- Self-actualized people are humble.

Despite all this, self-actualized people are not perfect. Bring no self-judgement to the number of statements you ticked – all growth begins with self-awareness, so whatever your 'tick-count' you now have greater self-awareness. We've touched on some of the points already, and by the time you've worked your way through the book, you will have covered them all. By then you'll be happy to let your true inner self shine through regardless of social etiquette, or dress code.

HABITS
Almost half of our behaviours are repeated daily. These are the hidden habits that underpin our existence, so if we want to Own Life, we have to own our habits.

The Subtle Power of Habit
Scientists say that habits emerge because the brain is always looking for energy-saving initiatives and habits mean the electronic pulses of the brain can follow well-trodden pathways[8].

Once a pattern is established, the synaptic connections are strong, and the brain can take a break from decision-making. Even if you successfully interrupt the pattern, the habit is literally encoded in the brain, ready to return when you let your guard down.

Try this right now. Put your hands out in front of you and interlock the fingers; notice which thumb is on top. Now take them apart and put them back together with the other thumb on top. How does that feel? Weird, right? You've formed a habit of doing it one way, you have no idea when that habit started and didn't even realize you had it until you just noticed it. Some people have the same habit as you, while others have the exact opposite.

To change a habit feels weird, and you naturally want to return to what feels normal. But if you keep noticing, keep practising the new way, then over a relatively short period, the new way becomes the habit, and it would be strange to ever go back again.

Reflect & Write: Consider your day so far in real detail from the moment you awoke. What have you done on autopilot? Can you identify 10, 15, even 20 things you have done without questioning them?

Helpful and Unhelpful Habits

Some habits are simply part of our routine – they don't bring real benefits or really get in the way. We tie our left shoe before our right or brush the upper left teeth before the lower left. We pick up the same brand of ketchup and open the curtains. We're simply efficient – reserving brain 'thinking capacity' for when it's needed later in the day. However, many habits have a much more profound impact on our lives. Some you may consider positive, and some you'd consider having a negative impact.

Reflect & Write: Make a list of 10 helpful and 10 unhelpful habits.

How Habits Form

Researched by MIT, and simplified by Duhigg[9], the neurological loop at the core of every habit consists of three parts: cue, routine and reward.

The routine is the behaviour (for example, checking my phone the moment I wake up, and then browsing it for 20 minutes). This routine first formed to satisfy a need for something, it was initially rewarding, and may continue to satisfy a craving. (My phone-checking habit started when I first installed Facebook and got a glorious shower of self-esteem endorphins every time I got a like, or someone accepted or sent a friend request. I was craving

acceptance, friendship, love, and feared rejection.)

The Cue starts the habit loop. Almost all cues fit into one of five categories: location, time, emotional state, other people, or immediately preceding action[10]. Working through the phone-checking example, it takes a little thought to isolate the real cue. It's not location because I do it wherever in the world I wake up. It isn't time because I do it regardless of what time my alarm is set for. I don't think it's my emotional state because it happens regardless of how I feel in the morning, and it happens whomever I wake up next to. So, it must be the immediately preceding action – waking from sleep. Now I have an autopilot loop which my conscious brain is giving no attention or energy to **cue** – awake; **routine** – I browse my phone; **reward** – I feel accepted.

How to Interrupt Habits and Form New Ones

To interrupt habits, we need to analyse the loop, starting with the current routine. This is the easy bit. The next job is to pin down the reward from the routine. What 'need' is this routine satisfying? What is the benefit? It is often a little more complex than you first imagine. 'I eat doughnuts to satisfy a hunger pang' may not be the whole truth! It may also be difficult if we've spent the past trying to deny that any benefits to the habit exist.

Take smoking. The reason people smoke, despite knowing

the harmful health impact of it, is because it genuinely satisfies some craving. Only if we can get really honest with ourselves about the benefit of an unhelpful habit, can we begin to overcome it.

Once we understand the 'need' the routine is satisfying, it's possible to set up some experiments to check if a different routine would result in the same satisfying feeling. If smoking is about getting away from the computer screen for five minutes and having a chat about something other than work, then would another routine have the same (or better) desired outcome?

Next, isolate the cue. Whenever the craving is first felt, log where, when, who with, how you're feeling, and what just happened. Hopefully, you'll begin to see a pattern.

Finally, have a plan and write it down. (Here's my plan to get over the compulsive early-morning phone checking: buy an alarm clock; leave my phone charging in the kitchen. Once I'm showered and dressed, use the time it takes to make and drink a coffee to browse my phone.)

The next activity will walk you through the process step-by-step and help you to be a habit changer for real!

Reflect & Write: Take your list of 10 unhelpful habits (see page 32). Which one would you most like to change?

- Write it as a goal statement: *My goal is to...*
- Consider when the goal is accomplished, and you've successfully removed the old routine from your life. What difference does this make to you? *The impact is...*
- What is the benefit of your current routine? What 'need' does it (or used to) satisfy? *The benefit is...*
- What alternative routine could you experiment with that may achieve the same benefit? *My new routine could be...*
- What is the cue that triggers the current routine (where,

when, who, emotional state, or preceding action)? *My cue is...*

- Knowing that the cue will arise again in the future, and the same need requires satisfying, what plan do you have for a new routine? *I plan to...*

Now it's time to put that plan into action. Make notes on the result of your experiment. If things don't go perfectly at first, how will you adapt the plan until you are successful?

That's one habit tackled; but remember, the synaptic connections for the old habit are strong, and you may find yourself falling backwards from time to time. This is normal. It takes perseverance to make the changes really, truly, stick.

You have identified another nine unhelpful habits. But one is enough for now. Shifting a habit isn't easy. Once you have the most important one locked down, return to the habit-changing process and tackle bad habit number two (put a note in your calendar for three months).

Reflect & Write: You already have 10 positive habits. Which new ones would you like to add? Make a list of five, and then select the one that feels like the easiest to achieve.

- Write a precise goal sentence and the reason why it is important to you: *I would like to (the new routine)... because (the benefit it brings)...*
- Now get really precise about the trigger for you to put the new habit into action, what is the cue? (Remembering: when, where, who, emotional state, preceding event). *My cue is...*
- Write a list of all the things that could possibly prevent it from happening. What can you do to mitigate each one of them? How can you prepare for the moment in advance? *What could get in my way, but I'll try not to let it...*

Keep a note of your progress for the next 21 days. Did you do it? If not, what got in the way? If yes, how do you feel about it?

Once you have the easiest one sorted, and it happens on autopilot (i.e. it takes no conscious effort to make it happen), then move to the next easiest. Oh, and celebrate. Nice job – you are on your way to Owning Life, and, you've proved to yourself that you can establish new positive habits.

SELF-CONTROL

Based on years of psychological research, Baumeister & Tierney[11] identified two traits that consistently predict 'positive life outcomes': intelligence and self-control.

Resisting the Marshmallow

When you listed all the things that could get in the way of you achieving the new habit, some will be external to you, and some will be internal. Did you have 'lack of willpower' on your list? It's perhaps the most common one.

In the early 1960s at Stanford University's Bing Nursery School, psychologist Walter Mischel gave children a choice between one reward (like a marshmallow, pretzel, or mint) they could eat immediately and a larger reward (two marshmallows) for which they would have to wait, alone, for up to 20 minutes. Years later, Mischel and his team followed up with the Bing preschoolers and found that children who had waited for the second marshmallow generally fared better in life.

Reflect & Write: Marshmallows might not be your thing, so list five areas where you believe greater willpower would be useful for you.

What Is Willpower?

Willpower is the ability to delay immediate gratification for the sake of positive future benefits. It has profound long-term consequences for health and wellbeing, and EVERYONE wants more of it!

The emotional brain is predisposed to exaggerate the value of immediate rewards and to severely discount the value of delayed rewards. The consequence is a natural over-prioritization of the short term over the long term, and a willpower challenge.

Having willpower strategies enables you able to balance the value of the rewards. You're able to push away short-term temptation in space and time (removing its immediate reward-giving powers), and bring distant rewards closer (both literally and metaphorically). Those that have established these strategies as habits could be labelled as 'having willpower', while those that don't employ the strategies may self-declare, 'I am impulsive'.

Like a muscle, willpower becomes fatigued with overuse, but it can be strengthened through training. Willpower isn't

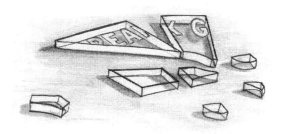

genetic, and the strategies employed to develop greater self-control can be learnt. You can grow your willpower, and the following tips can help.

Strengthening Your Willpower Muscle

Tip 1 might surprise you. There is a direct correlation between glucose levels and willpower[12], when we're hungry, not only are we likely to be grumpy, we have less control over thoughts, emotions, impulse and focus. So eat! Properly! Sugar could bring a helpful short-term boost of willpower, but leads to sugar-crash and potentially, longer-term health problems. Go for foods with a low glycaemic index (GI) since the body converts them into glucose more slowly, and therefore produces a more sustainable performance level – think protein, vegetables, raw fruit, and nuts.

Tip 2 is equally underwhelmingly basic, (which could be either disappointing or pleasing to you). When you're tired, sleep!

Tip 3 takes us back to your simple daily habits. By trying to make a change to something super-simple, you begin to give the willpower muscle a daily workout.

Tip 4 relates to knowing we only have a limited supply of willpower, (it gets depleted throughout the day and recharged overnight), so the smartest strategy is to reduce how much you need by removing temptation. Instead of salivating and using the force of will to resist the marshmallow while staring at it, the kids that showed the best long-term results were those that turned away from it and did something completely different to distract themselves, effectively taking the tempting marshmallow out of the room. The people who believe they have strong willpower, are actually those who exert it least often (and therefore have it in reserve for when it's really needed). So, distance yourself from temptations that deplete your willpower reservoir.

Exercising willpower in one aspect of life has the wonderful natural consequence of greater willpower in other aspects without apparently trying. For example, working hard to stick to a gym routine may also be rewarded with less impulsive spending, greater focus at work and a tidier home.

Reflect & Write: Consider a task that you always complete with your dominant hand – for example, using a spoon or brushing your teeth. Now use your other hand instead. Or try something more difficult; notice your speech patterns and how you insert 'filler' words or sounds, like 'erm', 'you know', 'like', and then begin to moderate your talking speed so you can eliminate them. What will you try? Write it down, and then give it a go.

Reflect & Write: Consider five things you use willpower to resist that form part of your daily life. How can you remove the need to exert willpower by removing temptation?

Exerting Self-control

Reflect & Write: Now let's bring a specific topic into sharp focus. If you could bring self-control to a single aspect of your life, what would it be?

- *My self-control focus is...*
- Now let's set a realistic but stretching goal for it. Making sure that there is a timeframe attached to it: *My goal is to...*
- What is the benefit of achieving this goal? Consider the

long term and the short term: *The benefit to my life is...*
The benefit to me every week of my life is...

- Next, make a plan. Exactly how will you approach achieving this goal? *I plan to...*

Reflect & Write: When will you review your progress? Write down your review date. When the date arrives, note down EVERYTHING you have done that has broken the old habit, and be proud of having done it. Next, consider the gap between your actual behaviour and the original plan. What have you learnt?

It's unlikely that you've completely smashed it on one hit, but you've learnt a bunch of things you didn't know when you set the original plan, which puts you in a better place to make a better plan.

Reflect & Write: Complete this sentence: *Based on my lessons, my new and improved plan is to...*

GROWTH MINDSET
Stripping back the work of Stanford University psychologist Carol Dweck into its most fundamental essence: A shift from 'I can't', to 'I can't yet' opens up a world of possibilities.

Fixed vs Growth Mindsets
All scientific 'laws' are actually hypotheses waiting to be disproved. And so is most of life, but we tend to believe that things are more fixed than they are. Until they change. And the same is true for you.

One of the most basic beliefs we carry about ourselves has to do with how we view and inhabit what we consider to be our personality. In Carol Dweck's book, *Mindset*[13], she defines a 'Fixed Mindset' as one that 'assumes that our character, intelligence, and creative ability are static givens, which we can't change in any meaningful way'. Any success that comes is a reinforcement of the natural talents we are born with, rather than the result of striving. Individuals with a fixed mindset seek and repeat those activities that have a high probability of success (since it reinforces 'smartness'), and the prospect of failure is avoided at all cost (since it would indicate an insurmountable flaw in character).

A 'growth mindset', on the other hand, thrives on challenge and sees failure not as evidence of an inbuilt deficiency but as an opportunity for growth. Those with a growth mindset believe that they can get smarter, more creative, and more talented by putting in time and effort.

Since our early years, we have a bias towards one mindset or the other, which impacts our relationship to failure and, ultimately, our capacity for happiness.

Which Are You?

How many of the following statements can you wholeheartedly say 'yes, that's soooo me'? Tick or cross them:

- I go after my dreams.
- I strive for progress, not perfection.
- Learning is my superpower.
- I am brave enough to try.
- I ask for help when I need it.
- I always strive to do my best.
- I seek new and difficult challenges.
- When I fail, I try again.
- I am a problem-solver.
- I stick with things and don't give up easily.

If your page is full of ticks, you're more likely to have a growth mindset. More crosses suggest that you currently tend to have a fixed mindset. Somewhere in between means there's plenty still to work on!

I Can't

Let's acknowledge that there are a whole bunch of things you can't do. I'll start you off with a list that jumps into my head within 10 seconds:

I can't speak French, run a marathon, stop craving coffee, grow younger, remember names, move to another country, afford to take six months off to travel the world, live my kids' lives for them, remember to floss every day, engage well on social media, fix a particularly bad relationship.

Reflect & Write: Go on, I've shared mine, your turn. What's on your list? Write down at least 10.

je ne peux
parler français

I Can't... Yet

Did your parents ever say to you 'There's no such thing as "can't",' Well, without the benefit of Carol Dweck's research budget, they were hitting the nail on the head. As simple as it sounds, and despite the waves it is making in the world of education, a growth mindset boils down to putting a single word at the end of a very common sentence – *I can't... yet.*

Go back to your list above and write 'yet' at the end of

every statement. There will be some that don't make sense so cross those ones off (I genuinely can't grow younger). There may be items on your list that would be undesirable even if you could do them, so they can go too (I really shouldn't want to live my kids' live for them). There may be some on your list that is low priority (I can't speak French, but I don't feel it's holding me back).

What remains is the important stuff, and with the word 'yet' added, it can feel quite liberating. I *can* learn to play the guitar, I *can* develop the capacity to speak in public, I *can* beat my craving, I *can* learn to remember names. I simply haven't executed the right strategies, or found the right teacher, or made it a priority, or persevered when things were difficult. All of which can be fixed.

Experimenting with a Growth Mindset

After learning the theory, I put it into practice. First, I visited a primary school in East London and was shown paintings the class had made, using photos of themselves dressed up as kings and queens to copy from. I saw what I'd expect to see – faces, crowns, gowns – the primary elements of the photos. But, not stopping there, the class adopted a growth mindset.

They gave themselves some feedback – what three things did they notice that were different between their painting and the original photo. Then they took feedback from their teacher, and finally from a six-year-old classmate. They had a second attempt at the painting. Then there was a second round of feedback and a third attempt at the painting. The whole process took only two weeks, and yet if you'd asked me to guess the ages of the children who painted the third pictures, I'd have said they were many years older.

Applying the process I learnt from six-year-olds, I challenged the story that I'd been telling myself for decades, the one that said, 'I can't draw.' For the first time ever, I had a real go at drawing something to the best of my abilities. I drew my son – and here is my first attempt. I was quite proud of it and could have stopped there.

But I'd visited the six-year-olds, so I applied the growth

mindset, received feedback in a grateful way, believed I could improve, and gave it a second attempt. Again, I was pleased with the outcome and impressed with the progress I had made. And could have stopped. But I'd seen the evidence of the impact of a third attempt at the primary school. After another round of feedback, I drew this picture of my daughter.

For 41 years, I believed I couldn't draw because I wasn't born with a talent. Now I know I can draw, and it wasn't talent that I'd previously lacked, it was self-belief and effort. The process only took three weeks, and I'm now more open to challenging my other long-held negative self-perceptions too. Over the next few pages, we'll be helping you to bring a growth mindset to your current limiting beliefs.

EFFORT OVER TALENT
Mastery

The '10,000 hours of practice' concept can be traced back to a 1993 research paper written by Anders Ericsson[14] and made popular in Malcolm Gladwell's book *Outliers*[15]. Ericsson's findings, which are not universally agreed on, were that individuals who have a talent for a specific discipline were overtaken by individuals with less natural talent but a better attitude towards practice. Even further – anyone could become a world expert at anything if they practice diligently for 10,000 hours, regardless of initial talent.

While we could spend energy trying to unpick the research methodology, it points to a common phrase that's often forgotten, 'practice makes perfect' (which I'd prefer to adapt to 'practice makes progress'). Without needing to read research papers, we can all agree that the more time we invest practising something, the better we get.

Reflect & Write: Look back to the strengths exercise from page 11 – write down five that you have at least a moderate level of competence at. Rate yourself 0–10, where 0 is 'I am a complete novice', 10 is 'I could be considered the best in the world at it'. I'm guessing that you're scoring between 5s and 8s. At some point in your life, you were at 0 for each one of these things, and you are now on the way to mastery. Next to each strength, write down how you became good at it.

Your notes now contain the strategies you have employed to achieve mastery. They may include perseverance, a great teacher, openness to feedback, self-awareness, acceptance that failure is part of the learning process, dedication, focus, prioritization, resilience, taking one step at a time, desire.

For some of your strengths, you remain on a steep learning curve – so keep doing what you are doing. For others, your level of expertise may have begun to 'flatline' – you are no longer improving.

Reflect & Write: Choose one from the list that has a high number yet has 'flatlined'. Imagine that you could be the best in the world at that thing (or simply the best person that you know of). What do you intend to do now to restart the process of mastery?

Start with a Single Step

You've just been thinking about how to get better at something that you're already good at; to keep raising the bar. For everything on that list, you started off as a complete novice. Your long journey to mastery started with a single (probably) wobbly step.

Reflect & Write: Go back to your list of 'I can't' statements. Choose one that you'd really be proud to be able to say 'I can' to and one that would make a difference to your professional life. Start your sentence *with I can't...'* and end it with … *yet.*

You may currently score a 1 ('I can't do it'), and throughout your life, there will be very few things that will be a 10, or a 9, or even an 8. But if there's something that's holding you back in life that is below a 4 ('I'm not quite OK at it'), then it needs to be addressed if you are to Own Life.

How will you begin? It's unlikely to be with a giant leap from 1 to 5. It's micro-steps of confidence-building. Ask yourself:

What would cause me to feel slightly more confident at this thing? This becomes your very first action. So, when will you start? What does success look like at a 2? Don't look beyond and define your goal based on you being a 7 – start by being realistic. Only when you've reached a 2, ask yourself what could cause me to feel slightly more confident? What does success look like at a 3? And what baby step will I take next?

Reflect & Write: Write down the very first baby step that you plan to take.

By the way, success at step 1 is simply to have given something a go. Bring no judgement to the outcome – you've broken a habit of not doing it, and you deserve a medal simply for giving it a go. Regardless of the external result, you are growing internally.

Concluding Thoughts

Change is inevitable, but habits put a brake on things. You truly can choose what an enhanced version of yourself looks like, and you really can develop the skill of self-control. It takes effort to change, and you'll hit difficulties. But you've already shown remarkable resilience and an ability to overcome challenges. The evidence is that you're here, investing time in your personal growth. What gets in the way most often is irrational – your emotional state of mind. In the next chapter, you'll discover how to overcome feelings like doubt, disappointment, frustration and guilt.

CHAPTER 3
MANAGING 'STATE'

If you were a robot, I could upload the program you designed in the last chapter and quick as a flash – you'd be upgraded. The new you instantly here! Instead, we have these inconvenient things called feelings that dance around bringing irrational inconsistency to our days. Thankfully however, it's possible to grow an appreciation for ALL the emotions we experience AND to experience a positive state of mind most of the time.

In the words of prolific author Dan Millman: *'You don't have to control your thoughts; you just have to stop letting them control you.'*

EMOTIONS
Appreciation for Our Human-ness
Have you seen the Disney film *Inside Out,* in which 11-year-old Riley's idyllic life comes crashing down around her when her family moves from Minnesota to San Francisco? The majority of the film is shot inside her head – following characters (the five main emotions) which are controlling her moods and actions: Joy, Sadness, Anger, Disgust, and Fear. Initially, all the characters want Joy to be in control – but the reality is that at various moments, other characters

step up to run things. Sadness enables Riley to connect with empathy to her old imaginary friend (Bing Bong), Fear keeps her alive, Anger gets her motivated, and Disgust is the signal that something is deeply offensive or distasteful.

Every one of us has a range of emotions that arise within us, and no-one lives a life of pure joy. Yet many of us have this quest in life to 'simply be happy' – it's a holy grail, and paradoxically, it's the quest that gets in the way of Owning Life. By accepting that 'negative' emotions exist and building an appreciation for psychological discomfort, we can develop 'distress tolerance' – and this is a leading predictor of life success.

Borrowing from the book *The Upside of your Darkside*,[16] *'People who use the full range of their natural psychological gifts are the most healthy, and often, the most successful... The most unwanted negative experiences end up shaping some of the most memorable events of our lives.'*

Anger does not have to turn to rage and violence. It can bubble up when we perceive an encroachment on our rights and stir us to defend ourselves and others and maintain boundaries.

Embarrassment is an early warning sign of humiliation; a signal that we've made a small mistake and that a small correction is required. Guilt is a signal that we're violating our moral code and therefore need to adjust our actions (or our code).

To experience a range of emotions is human, and natural, and important. You may wish for endless days of sunshine, but nature knows better; it's only because of the bad-weather-days that we have an environment to enjoy when the clouds clear. So instead of attempting to deny 'negative' emotions and wishing for constant joy, how can you celebrate the colourful lessons that the full repertoire brings?

Gratitude for Emotions

Below is a list of emotions, see if you can recall a specific moment in your life when you have felt each one:

- Hurt
- Angry
- Selfish
- Hateful
- Critical
- Sceptical
- Jealous
- Frustrated
- Distant
- Confused
- Rejected
- Helpless
- Insecure
- Anxious
- Inadequate
- Discouraged
- Embarrassed
- Overwhelmed
- Guilty
- Ashamed
- Depressed
- Lonely
- Bored
- Tired
- Remorseful
- Stupid
- Inferior

- Isolated
- Content
- Relaxed
- Thoughtful
- Intimate
- Loving
- Trusting
- Thankful
- Serene
- Faithful
- Confident
- Important
- Appreciated
- Respected
- Worthwhile
- Proud
- Successful
- Surprised
- Hopeful
- Optimistic
- Cheerful
- Creative
- Energetic
- Excited
- Fascinated
- Daring

I encourage you to pause on each word and find some stillness to allow your memory to bring specific moments back to the surface.

If you did just pause and allow yourself to daydream, then you will have been on a wonderfully rich journey in your mind. As you brought past experiences to mind, you may have also been reliving the past emotions too – and their physical symptoms. As you run through the list, if you really stopped to contemplate a specific situation, you are likely to also now feel how you felt back when the moment happened. At moments, did you notice the heart race? A slight blush? A deep sigh? A smile at the corner of your mouth? An involuntary tightening of some muscles?

You see, our minds and bodies are connected, and this can work either for or against us. We'll explore how, later in this chapter.

Reflect & Write: If I gave you the option to cross out 50 per cent of the list of emotions, and live without ever experiencing those emotions again, would you? What could the long-term negative consequences be of never feeling them again?

E-motion

Originally from the Latin word *emovere* (to move), it wasn't until the early 19th century that the word 'emotion' became attached to feelings, and now we can consider that emotion is 'energy in motion'.

When you recall any one of the above emotions – the moment you felt it most strongly, you were also feeling pretty alive (perhaps except for boredom). Even with serenity, while there's unlikely to be a great deal of visible high energy, there is an internal intensity to it.

Try it now. Select one of the words – choose a positive

emotion (because it's just more fun!) Really bring to mind the last time that you felt it deeply. Close your eyes, count the next three breaths, and then transport yourself back in time. Pay attention to what you notice, tuning into all of your senses of sight, sound, smell, taste and touch. Allow the emotion to rise up, completely immersing your entire body in its light. Then just sit with it and enjoy reliving this positive moment.

Whenever you feel ready, bring yourself back to this moment, and tune into the bodily sensations associated with this emotion. Precisely where in your body do you feel it, and precisely how does it feel? Allow this spot to hold your full attention. Notice how the sensation changes and another part of your body calls for attention – allow your awareness to be moved by the changing sensations in your body.

Whenever feels right, open your eyes, and recount what you felt.

Did you notice that it was dancing around? The energy is in motion, right? It never stays the same, it never stays still. It peaks and it troughs, it tingles, it aches, it is intense, it is teasingly faint. It is all those things, and it will never be exactly the same again.

You've been focussed on a short period when a single emotion was present. If you zoom out and consider a week – perhaps the last week, how many different emotions did you experience? Maybe not many in an I'll-remember-that-moment-for-the-rest-of-my-life way – but I'll bet that if you are really tuned into the ebb and flow of what's going on inside, you'll experience 50 per cent of the emotions listed above every week. Emotions come and go, like clouds. It may look bleak and overcast, as though there is no end to the greyness, and yet you realize some time later that the clouds have thinned, or parted, or completely disappeared.

The challenge we face is that when we see blue skies and try to hold onto a positive emotion like joy, we immediately begin to imagine the loss of this 'positive' emotion and therefore wake ourselves up from the pleasurable experience.

On the other hand, when the skies are grey, we might imagine that there is no end in sight. It is often the worry that things will remain grey, that causes us more suffering than the actual emotion itself. So, remember, behind the clouds is a blue sky and it will always emerge. Emotion is energy in motion – so simply give it the freedom to move.

Changing the Climate

Having acknowledged that a great range of emotions come and go, you may also have a prevailing climate – a tendency for the arid conditions of the Sahara, or tropical rains in the equatorial heat, or the six months of darkness followed by six months of light at the Poles. Just as it is possible to take a holiday to a different part of the world, it is also possible to take emotional vacations and even completely change your emotional climate for good. We're just about to learn how.

WHO IS IN THE DRIVING SEAT?

How Many of You Are There?

Set a timer for four minutes. Simply sit with your eyes closed in a quiet space. Feel your breath rise and fall. When you notice a thought arise in your mind, count it and return to your breath and wait. When you notice another thought, count two. And so on.

How many thoughts arose in your mind? Did you become attached to any of them, whisked away on a journey that you hadn't intended? Did you choose to have those thoughts? If not, who did? And if you were the person

having the thought, who was doing the counting?

We have 100,000 thoughts per day, 95 per cent of which can be classified as negative or limiting. You see, you're completely normal, just like everyone else. We are wired this way, and it's one of the many reasons homo sapiens are top dogs.

Emotional Reactions

Our emotions are constantly flowing. This started when we were babies. We were bathed in love, and it felt good. We were shouted at, and it felt bad. Before we had any words to describe our feelings, we were connecting an external stimulus to an internal feeling. And this happens over and over and over again. It becomes autopilot, sometimes we don't know why we feel the way we feel – we just do. The association between an event and a feeling is hardwired deep in our subconscious.

In one experiment, images flashed on a screen in front of a group of volunteers who had electrodes attached to their palms to monitor changes in sweat (an indicator of stress). The images flashed up quicker and quicker – and all contained positive pictures: people smiling, cute dogs, a chocolate bar. The images changed even more quickly, so much so that the participants could no longer tell what each image was before the next one appeared. Within this set of images was a single shot of a scary hairy spider. It was on screen for micro-seconds, and none of the volunteers could recall seeing it. Yet their sweat response indicates that they did.

Who is in the driving seat? Your body can react to seeing something you don't even know you saw!

When you turned over to this page, before you saw any words, you saw the illustration. You may not have paused sufficiently to notice your internal reaction to it – but there probably was one.

It may still be with you now, even subtly. While you've been reading these words, it sits there in your peripheral vision. A sea of expectant eyes, a lack of smiles, and more people who you can't even make out in the background. A prepared script, a microphone ready to pick up your faltering voice, spotlights exposing the beads of sweat on your brow. Five paces to almost certain humiliation and the end of any chance of a normal life.

Public speaking, the number-one fear.

Notice any body sensations now? You know that you're not about to give that speech – but perhaps your body is starting to shift into fight or flight mode.

Who is in the driving seat? Your body issues distress

signals and you may feel anxious despite knowing there is no real threat.

What is more, as we notice the physical sensations, we attach meaning to them: 'My hands are sweaty, I must be nervous about something. What is there to be nervous about?' So you come up with something that makes sense of the sensation. If we asked the spider volunteers if they felt nervous about something, and if so, what – none would say a spider, but most would come up with some different justification.

Sometimes a thought arises, and we then feel an emotion about that thought. Sometimes it's the opposite; an emotion arises, and we attach thought to it. These two systems are a result of the evolution of the human brain. Around the brain stem is the limbic system (sometimes referred to as the mammalian brain), which is responsible for generating emotions, and processing emotional memories. At the epicentre of this system is the amygdala, which is the first part of the brain to receive sensory information and is responsible for the automatic actions that ensure survival from external threats. Later in human evolution (and later in childhood brain development), come the frontal lobes that deal with planning, thinking, and regulating the emotional excesses of the limbic system. This area is activated much more slowly, is much less powerful, and as a result, we all occasionally struggle to keep our emotions from running our lives.

In his wonderful book, *The Chimp Paradox*[17], Professor Steve Peters accepts that no matter how hard we try to manage our inner chimp (our emotional self), it is completely normal to have occasional emotional outbursts, because this is simply the way the brain works. Of course, you should try to reduce the negative consequences of your behaviour, but then forgive yourself, you're not perfect (… yet!).

How effectively we manage the interplay between the limbic (emotions) and frontal (logical) systems largely determines our emotional intelligence (which in turn determines our success). We'll return to EI (emotional intelligence) later in the book.

INTERNAL RATHER THAN EXTERNAL
Mood Diary
To what extent is your mood affected by what's happening in the outside world?

Take an audit of the last half-day, walking through moment-to-moment, and make a 'mood diary' of how you felt and what triggered the feeling. For example

Time	Event	Mood
06:30	Alarm sounds	Tired yet inspired because I've got an exciting day ahead
06:44	Son wakes up a little earlier than usual	Nervous about how my wife feels at being woken up, some sadness that my morning meditation has been interrupted
06:45	Sound of the toilet flushing	Happy that my son has taken himself to the toilet without disturbing anyone
06:50	Son says, 'Cuddles Daddy.'	Love – I won't see him for a while

07:00	Daughter enters the kitchen not wearing her school uniform	Love and suppressed mild disappointment that she hasn't got dressed
07:30	Wife books a social event with friends which clashes with the weekend I'd been planning to take her away for a surprise present	Disappointment, frustration, annoyance, sadness, then guilt after displaying my annoyance
07:45	Daughter picks up her phone and does her 'times tables' app, beating her high score	Pride, satisfaction, contentedness
08:00	Opening bedroom curtains at the front of the house to blue skies and sunshine	Happiness, gratitude

Reflect & Write: Do your own audit now.

What a journey we go on when we really stop to notice it. Most of the time we'd simply get an overall sense of things, and describe the average, i.e. it was a good, bad, or alright morning.

External events trigger internal emotional reactions, which impact your state – this state affects how you encounter the world, and how you respond to it. The extent to which external events impact your internal state is manageable and varies from person to person.

Who do you know that seems to float above day-to-day events, they seem to have some kind of buffer zone protecting their moods?

The most emotionally in-control person I know is...

And who is the opposite – their mood is entirely driven by the most recent event or conversation that happened to them?

The most emotionally out-of-control person I know is...

Reflect & Write: If the first person is a 10 (completely able to manage their internal state), and the second person is 0 (their state depends on the external world), what's your number and why do you choose it?

Beliefs Colour External Events

An external event happens, and our emotions are triggered. But how is it that someone next to us, witnessing the same event, seems to feel differently about it?

Take a look at this photograph (credit Phil Noble[18]) Michael Owen (England's third-highest goal scorer and a Liverpool legend), has just missed a golden opportunity to score and win an important match in the dying seconds. Notice the common reaction – Michael's (lying on the floor) hands on his head, and all of his teammates, and every fan behind the goal all mimicking Michael, hands on their heads.

External event (missed shot), internal reaction (disappointment), automatic behaviour (hands on the head, and mouths wide open).

But look a little closer (it's like a *Where's Wally* challenge), can you spot two fans with raised fists, clearly in celebration. In colour, this photo shows these two fans are wearing yellow, in contrast to the red of the Liverpool fans. For them: external event (missed shot), internal reaction (elation),

automatic behaviour (fist raised, shout of triumph). You clearly see two different responses to the same external stimulus.

Why? In this case, it's obvious – they have different beliefs. One person believes that Liverpool is the best team in the world, the other that Manchester United are. Our beliefs and values alter our perception of an external event. As William Shakespeare famously wrote in *Hamlet*: *'Nothing is either good or bad, but thinking makes it so.'*

It turns out that our level of happiness has little to do with the environment in which we live, but our interpretation of it. Michael Neill[19] puts it nicely: *'we live in a world of thought, but we think we live in a world of external experiences'*. In other words, we often can't tell the difference between the world that we have constructed in our imagination and the real one. The mind projects what it sees onto the canvas of reality rather than acting as a camera to accurately record reality.

This means that we all make up stuff that simply isn't there (sound familiar?)! So remember, just because a thought is in your head, it doesn't mean it's true.

Different Experiences

Consider some recent examples from your life where your response differed from someone else's. There's no need to defend, justify or rationalise the different responses for now, simply acknowledge them.

Here's an example. Earlier this week, my wife, daughter and I walked past a scruffy young man huddled against the cold, clearly homeless, and begging for money. Here are the first words that each of us uttered:

Olive (my 10-year-old daughter): 'Mum, can we take him home and give him a shower?'

Tammy (my wife): 'Todd, do you have any money on you?'

Me: 'Society is so broken that it allows victims to sleep on the street.'

On our local Facebook group, the variety of responses increases: 'Why doesn't he get a job, the rest of us have to work?' 'He's the eyes and ears of the drug gangs.' 'He's collecting £150 per day, don't give him your cash.' 'The majority of homeless guys suffer from mental health illness, give the guy a break.' 'More than half the people begging on the streets of our town are not genuinely homeless'. 'Spare change or real change. Give your money to the homeless charity who make sure it gets well used for the right things.'

You see, we all walked along the same street and saw the same guy. But our emotional responses ranged from pity to anger, from contempt to sorrow.

Reflect & Write: Your turn. What recent sight, event, show, news headline, etc. caused you to have a different reaction to some people around you?

The 'World' Is Created in the Mind

It's sometimes quite easy to notice the symptoms of different perspectives, but what is the cause?

Our five senses receive four million bits of information every second, the vast majority of which don't enter our conscious awareness as it's simply impossible for us to process it all. For example, until I mention it, and you read these words, you're probably not aware of the physical sensation of your foot on the floor. But now you are aware. The sensory data was always there – your subconscious had taken the decision that this was unimportant information for you to know and had therefore deleted it.

All the time, you are deleting more than 90 per cent of the available sensory information – and unaware of what you're deleting. It simply isn't in your awareness. The person sitting next to you may have very similar sensory inputs but is deleting different information. Therefore, their experience of the same moment is different from yours. Our filters are based on values, beliefs, memories, personality, and attitude, and as we discovered in Chapter 1, they are as unique as your thumbprint.

These filters determine not only what we delete, but also how our minds distort things – misrepresenting reality and causing us to jump at shadows and 'see' evidence of a homeless man being involved in drug supply.

Finally, we have a 'generalization' filter – a process of learning and drawing conclusions so that information can be used again without having to go through a reanalysis every time we come across something similar. For example, phobias often result from a one-time event that has been generalized to be perceived as an every-time event. It is the brain process of generalization that causes us to make instant judgements about new people we meet based on our past experience with similar-looking people.

The end result of all this filtering is that we are not living in the real world, we are subconsciously creating a fantasy world that, to us, accurately represents the outer world. Yet it is distorted. We then have thoughts and emotions about this fantasy world rather than the real one; and these affect our behaviour, which in turn, shapes the world that we experience.

To some, a social occasion is full of opportunities to exchange stories with interesting people. If this is how you perceive an event, interesting conversations are likely to take place. However, for other people the same event is perceived as threatening, and perhaps an opportunity to be ignored by people who believe themselves to be more interesting. Hence this is what happens.

Sometimes known as the 'law of attraction', you get more of what you spend time thinking about, because without knowing it, you are creating it! So, to dial-up or down any emotion, you can choose to work on influencing your external environment or on your internal interpretation of the external world.

And it's the second option that allows you to Own Life. You *can* change your filters, and this is what we'll look at next.

PROGRAMMING THE MIND
Gratitude Habit

In a moment I want you to try something I learnt from inspiring public speaker Steve Head[20]. Look at the sums below, take a few seconds to digest them – and then say a single word out loud. Ready? Go.

$$1x1 = 1$$
$$2x2 = 4$$
$$3x3 = 9$$
$$4x4 = 15$$

Did you say 'wrong'?

In fact, 75 per cent of the sums are right, yet we're programmed to notice what's wrong. When there are no tea bags left in the cupboard, we moan, and it can set up a day of noticing everything wrong. The traffic, the weather, the temperature in the office, the pen clicking of the person next to us. Yet we rarely notice the 100 previous days when there was a tea bag in the cupboard.

Reflect & Write: A common filter that we carry is to notice the 15's (the things that go wrong in life), rather than the 1, 4, 9's (the good stuff). So, rebalance this for today by writing a long list of all the little things that have gone well.

Reflect & Write: Continuing from the last exercise, consider anything and everything that you are grateful for and write a list of at least 10 things (and keep on going if they keep on coming!).

How do you feel now? Probably, really good. This good feeling can have a lasting effect, and change your behaviour, which impacts your results, which makes you feel good. It's a positive cycle that starts with gratitude, and it's a wonderful habit to foster.

Every day, at the same time, take a pen and paper and write down three things that you are grateful for. Attempt never to repeat anything you've written before. Do this for 21 straight days and notice how you feel.

At the start of the practice, everything you write might feel like THE BIG STUFF: my family; a roof over my head; peace in my neighbourhood; food in the cupboard. But as you challenge yourself to come up with novel things to  write, you begin to appreciate the small stuff too. The buds appearing on the cherry tree; the dawn arriving minutes earlier each spring day; the feeling of calm when shaking off the work shoes in the evening; the little bird that hopped across your path and gave a merry tweet!

You may like to do this using pen and paper. I like to use an app, and it's about time I mentioned my favourite app of all time. It's the app I've recommended to more than 2,000 people and I believe that if you create the habit of sticking to it every day, then you're guaranteed to increase how much you Own Life. It's called the 'Five Minute Journal', by Intelligent Change Inc. Check it out on your phone right now. It will change your life.

In the morning, the five-minute journal first asks you to record three things you're grateful for. It then asks, 'what will I do to make today great?' This goes back to the earlier chapter about purpose – it's causing you to have an intention for your day. There's then a single line for you to write a daily affirmation. This is something that you are good at – it's turning 1,4,9 on yourself.

In the evening, there's a moment to reflect and record 'three amazing things that happened today'. This makes you replay the day in your mind, asking your brain to go searching for the highlights – and it's amazing how many there are when you really go looking. After a while, you'll begin to register these amazing things as they happen, thinking to yourself 'I might write that tonight.'

There's also space to record one photo. I now have a collection of hundreds of images – recording a highlight of every day of my last few years. It's such a joy to occasionally flick through them – an instant state shifter and smile generator. If you don't fancy the app, do what my daughter did, and fill a notebook.

The Computer

We learnt earlier how the limbic system (emotional brain) reacts quicker than the frontal system (rational brain) – and how we can be in the grips of emotion and reacting to it without feeling there is space between external stimulus and internal response. It's then very hard for your relatively weak rational brain to regain control.

The better strategy is to develop the antidote so that the emotional response doesn't activate in the first place. Steve Peters[21] refers to the parietal lobe of the brain as the computer, with two functions: to think and act automatically for you using programmed thoughts and behaviours; and as a reference source for information, beliefs and values. The parietal system (computer), works faster than either the limbic (emotional) or the frontal (rational) systems and therefore outperforms them both.

By programming the computer with useful autopilots, we can eliminate some negative emotion-driven behaviours. For example, when I'm driving and make way for someone to pass down a narrow street, and they don't bother to raise a hand in thanks, my immediate emotional response used to be anger (which could stay with me for a while and affect my driving.)

With the space to think and the benefit of hindsight, my rational brain has (over the years) caught up with this negative consequence to an external stimulus and programmed the computer not to respond negatively. Now, when the same situation occurs, my instant computer response is of calm, and my emotional response is joy, my behaviour is to smile as I remember that I am capable of managing my inner chimp.

The Body-mind Connection

Do you remember how when you recalled past positive experiences (see page 67), you felt an actual sensation in your body, and your posture may well have changed as a result? It works the other way around too. If you hold a slouchy, low energy posture, you will feel lethargic, unenthusiastic, bored. If you walk tall, stand upright, sit with a straight back – then you will feel more awake, more energized, more ready for life. The mind and body are connected, so let's see how we can use the body to affect our state.

Recall something that you are wonderfully proud of. Pause. Really remember it.

Now notice how the feeling of pride washes around your body, paying attention to any sensation in any particular part. Allow your posture to change so that the feeling of pride swells. Notice your breath rising and falling, and the sensation of your heart beating.

Insert some words into your feelings and say to yourself 'I feel strong.' And believe that you are.

Adjust your posture, so you feel physically firmer but without straining. Repeat the words 'I feel strong' and notice how your body naturally reacts to the words. We've created a congruent loop whereby body and mind are 'saying' the same thing. Capture the body feeling. Capture its shape in your memory, because in the future, by taking this posture, you will be triggering the connected emotions of strength and pride. This body strength will bring mental strength to your future challenges.

Strong Morning Habits

Consider the start of your day. The alarm goes off. What happens next? The first thought: 'It's too early, I need some more sleep, I'm comfy here, I've got a bit more time.' And the first action? Hit the snooze button. (I use my iPhone as my alarm, and the snooze button is 10 times the size of the stop button – Apple is willing me to hit snooze!) Then what? The alarm goes off again. A quick mental calculation, 'What's happening first thing? Can I afford another five minutes in bed?... Yes.' Second action? Hit snooze. Eventually, you can hit snooze no longer. 'Damn, I've really got to get up now.'

You drag yourself from beneath the safe comfort of your duvet and into a cold room, and switch on autopilot – coffee, breakfast, shower, coffee, search for clothes, search for keys, leave the house not a moment sooner than you have to, commute in a daze, arrive and begin the first interaction with colleagues: 'How are you? ... OK.' Coffee.

Would you consider this to be a strong start to your day? Is your posture when arriving at work glowing with strength and pride? What message are you giving to others as they interact with you?

Every day, at some point, if it's going to be a great day, you have to shift from this weak state to a strong one. You've established a poor habit – a deeply ingrained morning routine that requires daily willpower to overcome, and it's time to create a new one.

Even if you've got a voice that says 'I am not a morning person' it doesn't have to be on permanent repeat for the rest of your life. So how about switching to a growth mindset and changing your story right now? *'I'm not a morning person, yet.'*

Can you allow yourself to believe that change is possible? You wouldn't be reading this book if you didn't.

Rate your typical morning zero (weak) to 10 (strong) – where are you currently? *I rate myself a... because...*

Suspending judgement for a moment, if you could achieve a perfect 10, what impact would this have? *If I could start every morning wonderfully, then...*

Now create a plan for your strong morning start. Some things others have done, that may inspire you are: leave the phone in a different room, select a good track to wake up to, change your alarm sound, choose the clothes for tomorrow before bedtime, buy and prepare breakfast the night before, use the Five Minute Journal app, wake 15 minutes earlier and do something you enjoy, write down your good intention for the day, go to bed earlier and don't watch your phone in bed, buy a new lovely smelling shampoo.

Reflect & Write: Get creative, how could you get closer to a perfect 10? What new morning routine would you like to foster?

Now, remember all the work you've been doing on willpower. Looking at the list above, what can you do to remove temptation, and therefore reserve your self-control for later in the day? Set a target to keep doing the new routine for 21 days, because if you do, then this strong routine becomes your new habit and it will take more effort to break it than to stick to it. Ready to start the day well? If you do, then everything that comes afterwards will flow more easily. Go on. You can do it.

A Wake-up Call

Our negative morning mindset can begin very young – conditioned into us by parents. My daughter was always a good sleeper, and when she woke in the mornings, we'd hear her singing to herself in bed with quiet contentment. For several years, I was able to begin my morning on my terms, with a strong routine.

Until Wilbur, my son arrived on a frosty January morning in 2014.

He was the opposite. He wakes early, and for him, being awake meant that everyone else should be too – he was ready to start his day. The deal with my wife was that, before 5 a.m., she'd get up and settle him again. After 5 a.m., it was my job to quietly start the day. Only I wasn't ready to start my day!

I'd hear him, check the clock, curse that it was 5:05 a.m. and therefore my job, wander slowly to his room rubbing my eyes while knowing that if I didn't walk quickly, the whole house would be awake. As I entered my son's room he'd be standing up in his cot, 'Daddy, Daddy, Daddy,' he'd cheerfully chant.

'Son, why are you awake so early? Why can't you go back to sleep? Come on, give Dad a break!'

It was this way for many many months. Then I realized something. I was teaching people about the importance of beginning the day right, and yet every day my son was naturally starting his day strong – full of energy, full of inspiration, full of love, and joy, and smiles. The first thing he experienced was his dad telling him that he wasn't wanted right now, that he was somehow wrong to be ready for another amazing day on planet Earth.

He only had a vocabulary of a few words, and yet already he was learning that mornings should be rejected. Deep in his brain, I was responsible for joining up synapses that would be with him for life. It was a wake-up call – what brain connections would I like him to have?

So, I embarked on a programme of resetting my own morning habits – retraining my brain to have different thoughts – setting up my computer auto-response that is faster than my chimp. How could I enable my son to have a 10/10 morning? It takes time, and lots of false starts, but I can tell you that it is possible.

Now when I hear my son in the morning I am overcome with gratefulness – I have trained my brain to have an automatic first thought, 'I have a son, and he loves me, I am truly blessed.'

Strong Daily Habits

Now you've considered your morning routine, how about the rest of the day. What positive habits would you like to establish that keep you strong? Would any of the following be helpful:

- When asking someone 'How are you?' Pause, and wait for a response rather than continuing with your task.
- Create energising breaks to your work – plan to focus for 50 minutes and do something recharging for 10 minutes.
- Get outside at least once – perhaps a brisk walk at lunchtime.
- Consider your nourishment – eat healthy snacks throughout the day.
- Replace coffee with something else.
- Notice your posture at work. If you're slouched, then your output will be slouched. Would a different seat work better for you?
- Is your workplace tidy, and free from distraction?
- How can you make the most of your commute? Listen to a podcast on an interesting topic?

If it feels too big of a stretch to be like this all day take a leaf from Elbert Hubbard: *'Be pleasant until ten o'clock in the morning and the rest of the day will take care of itself.'*

Reflect & Write: Once you've started your day right, how would you like to continue it? Complete this sentence: *My days will be strong because I'm going to...*

EXPECTATIONS
The Happiness Equation
Mo Gawdat was a Google executive, successful in the trappings of life, but deeply unhappy. His quest for happiness led him to a simple equation:

$$Happiness = reality - expectation$$

He was severely tested when he lost his son to a routine operation at the age of 21.[22] When he talks about losing his son, Mo explains that nothing he could do, and no amount of crying could bring him back. He had to reset things. Make today, day zero. Then work each day to make it slightly better. We often wish the world was a certain way, no poverty, for example, or friendly smiles from colleagues – but when these wishes become unrealistic expectations, then we find the source of unhappiness.

What I take from Mo's advice is to have acceptance that the world is imperfect, unfair, and sometimes harsh. Therefore, when I come across an example of this, I'm not crushed by its emotional impact, but simply inspired by the belief that I have the potential to make the reality just slightly better.

Allowing Things to Simply 'Be'

What can you control?

Your own response to the external world, and nothing else. You may have some influence over what happens in your environment, or how other people behave, but you certainly can't control them.

Suffering happens, and if you have built an over-optimistic fantasy that it won't, you will live an 'if only' life. One in which the true events don't match your idealized imaginary ones.

Should you lower your expectations? Imagine that tomorrow will really be terrible, and then be happy when things are not as bad as you'd imagined? That doesn't feel like a recipe for happiness either. So, what's the answer?

Have hopes, have dreams, be inspired by how great tomorrow can be. Have expectations of how you will respond to external events but let go of any fantasy that tomorrow will match the world you've imagined. When a moment arises, allow it to be exactly as it is – without judgement, and take pride in your ability to maintain your state regardless of external stimulus.

Reflect & Write: When you are considering the next 48 hours, what expectations do you have? What range of possible scenarios exist – from the very worst to the very best? How could you respond to the extremes?

Now let go of expecting it to be wonderful or awful; chances are that it will fall between the two. But regardless of what transpires, you now know that your inner world doesn't have to reflect it.

It's in Your Mind

I recently watched a talk by Gen Kelsang Nyema (a Buddhist nun),[23] where she started by asking the audience three questions:

1. Are you having a good day?
2. Why? (what's behind your previous response?)
3. Tomorrow, would you rather have a good day or a bad day?

How would you respond to them? If you're like me, the answer to the final question is, of course, 'I want a good day'. But when you look at your response to the second question, what is it that you have listed as your reasons for today being good or bad? It's a list of things that happened, right! Circumstances you largely can't control. Therefore, you may wish for tomorrow to be good, but the reality is it's out of your control, leading to yo-yoing happiness.

We need to stop outsourcing our happiness to other people and events and blaming them for our unhappiness. We need to start cultivating a source of happiness that comes from the inside. We need to start Owning Life.

Happiness and unhappiness are states of mind, and therefore their real causes can't be found outside the mind. It isn't what is happening, it's how we respond to what's happening that determines happiness, and this comes from our state of mind.

How do we cultivate a reliable, peaceful state of mind? Right now, sit comfortably with your feet gently resting on the floor and notice the movement of your breath through your nostrils, and soften your gaze so the world becomes blurred while just about being able to read these words.

Breathe out agitation, any busyness or frustration as if it

was dark smoke.

Breathe in clear, bright light, the nature of inner peace, imagining it filling your entire body and mind.

As you continue to notice the sensation of your breathing, imagine the dark smoke leaving every pore in your body and being replaced by clear, bright light.

Now just sit and enjoy the inner peace that arises. Be patient. Give yourself some time right now to just pause.

When you are ready to move on, feel determined to bring this inner peace into the rest of your day.

Meditation is the mental action of concentrating on a peaceful, positive state of mind and can be as simple as the few minutes you have just experienced. Load this simple technique into your brain's parietal (computer) system by fostering it as a daily practice, and then notice how easy it is to have a good day, every day.

Concluding Thoughts

At any moment in time, we can pause, turn our attention inwards and enquire about our current state of mind. We can't always rationalize why it is the way it is, or why we feel different from other people who seem to be in similar situations. Your emotions will ebb and flow every moment of life, and you really wouldn't choose it any other way. You can experience an inner smile more often by cultivating positive morning routines and daily gratitude. Next, we'll tackle some of the more difficult emotions, but before launching into all that, allow the edges of your mouth to turn up a little – give yourself an inner grin.

CHAPTER 4
FEAR, FAILURE AND GRIT

Fear can prevent you from living the life of your dreams. I know this is true for you because it's true for everyone. So feel OK about this, you are completely normal.

In her famous book *Feel the Fear and Do It Anyway,* Susan Jeffers[24] explains that in most cases the inability to deal with fear is not a psychological problem; it is one that the mind can be educated to overcome. In this chapter, you will learn how to push through resistance and begin to take control of the future.

WHAT ARE YOU AFRAID OF?
Stepping Back

Have you ever been in a classroom with a tutor, or perhaps a meeting with a boss and a fair few other people and the discussion is energized and interesting, and fast flowing. As the debate develops, you get a thought. A good thought. It may be a question, a comment, a challenge, a reference. It's something that could really change the direction of the conversation. It really is a very very good thought. While the conversation continues around you, you begin to get excited, you feel it in your stomach. You begin to rehearse in your mind what you will say, and what other brilliant ideas you can link to it. Your thoughts continue as you begin to re-engage with what's happening in the room. Space arises, no one is talking, and it's the perfect moment for you to insert your idea. You know this is the moment.

And you do nothing.

You let the moment pass. You haven't contributed your potential, and the discussion is weaker for it. Luckily, someone else in the room makes the exact same point. And everyone else pats them on the back, 'What a great comment!' And inwardly you're thinking, 'That was my point.' Outwardly you may say, 'I was going to say that!' The question is, what stopped you from stepping forward?

Fear. It wasn't there when you had the initial thought but grew from a tiny seed into a rampant tree within your own mind, although nothing had changed in the external environment. But fear of what? In this case, something called sociophobia (the fear of making a fool of yourself in front of other people – 'is my thought actually silly?'). It's the most common phobia. Included within its sphere are public speaking, talking to strangers, networking and new groups of people.

Fear Spotting

Reflect & Write: You too may occasionally suffer from sociophobia and can recognize the anxiousness it generates. What other things cause you to feel anxious? Let's collect all of them now, how long a list can you generate?

Reflect & Write: In the sociophobia example above, the fear of being judged causes people not to speak up. What are you not doing because you feel anxious?

You see, your fears are holding you back. If you allow yourself to dream of a wonderful future, of achieving all of your potential, and being wonderfully successful, then the butterflies automatically start. You will never eradicate fear for as long as you are exposed to something new and different (which is almost daily!). So we can all stop trying to remove fear from our lives – IT IS NOT GOING TO HAPPEN. Through this chapter, you will learn to understand the nature of fear, and how to release yourself from its powerfully limiting grip.

Everyone Is Afraid

It may be reassuring to know that some of the fears you just wrote about are very common. Did you have any of these themes coming up? Tick any that apply to you:

1. I don't like to try radically new things (fear of uncertainty).
2. I'm not really good enough, and I will be found out (fear of inadequacy).
3. I wish things could stay the way they are (fear of change).
4. My life is passing me by (fear of missing out).

5. If I try, I may not succeed (fear of failure).
6. I may look stupid (fear of being judged).
7. People may not like me (fear of rejection).

If you could take a look at 100 notebooks, you'd find that the majority of the above statements are ticked for the majority of people. Why is this the case? Surely the human species could have evolved to eliminate these limiting thoughts? Keep reading, and soon you will be thankful that the opposite is true.

Homo Sapiens

Like all animals, human beings have evolved ways to help protect ourselves from danger. Our senses constantly scan for signs of danger, and these inputs are sent directly to the amygdala (the almond-shaped set of neurons existing in all vertebrates), which tells the body to respond automatically, and instantly (before the rational human brain catches up – remember this from Chapter 3?).

Two systems are activated: the sympathetic nervous system uses nerve pathways to initiate responses in the body, and the adrenal-cortex system uses the bloodstream.[25] The combined effect of these two systems is the fight-or-flight response, and cause changes in the body that include:

- Heart rate and blood pressure to increase.
- Pupils dilate to take in as much light as possible.
- Veins in the skin constrict to send more blood to the major muscle groups (sometimes described as 'chilling' as a result of the hands and feet feeling cold).
- Blood-glucose level increases.
- Some muscles tense as they are energized

by adrenaline and glucose (responsible for goosebumps).

- Other muscles to relax to allow more oxygen into the lungs (which can also affect bladder control).
- Nonessential systems (like digestion) shut down to allow more energy to be directed to the emergency functions.
- Trouble focussing on small tasks (the brain is directed to focus only on the big threats).

When faced with a physical threat, these automatic responses help us to survive. For the 10,000 years of homo sapiens' evolution, it is this feature of our brains that kept our ancestors alive and is the reason we exist today. I am grateful that the automatic fear response has survived the process of human evolution!

Modern-day Emotional Threats

When your ancestors began to migrate from the African plains, they faced daily physical threats, and you too may occasionally face real physical dangers in which case these body responses are helpful.

We also frequently face psychological threats. Turn back to the image on page 57, you are about to give a very important speech. The audience is settling down in their seats. They include your colleagues, your boss, and all the important people in your academic field, your friends and family, and a considerable number of the public who have paid to hear you talk. The microphone has been tested, the audience goes quiet, and the compere introduces you. Five paces away, up a handful of steps is the podium, and a sea of eyes all turned in your direction. The chatter in the room subsides to leave a hush of anticipation; the next voice to be heard by the entire congregation will be yours.

Reflect & Write: As you imagine this scenario, notice how you are feeling. Write down the sensations that you are noticing in your body right now.

Do you actually feel those sensations as you sit here reading this sentence? They aren't imagined. The feelings are real, right here, right now even though the scenario is made up. You are not actually going to give that presentation, your rational brain knows this, but your amygdala has reacted and set into motion all the symptoms of fight-or-flight. The body responds to emotional threats, be they real or not, and you can't prevent it from happening.

Our goal is therefore to accept the facts of evolution and instead create strategies the rational brain can use to either reduce the negative impact of the body's stress response or cause it to be activated less frequently. Where there is no physical threat, our goal is to reduce the distracting noise caused by the body so that the rational brain can simply get on with performing its job.

PUSHING THROUGH FEAR

I Just Can't Handle It

Look at the list of fears you made on page 82. If we added your list to mine, and to my daughter's, and that of everyone else reading this book, we'd end up with a very long list of things to fear. These things are likely to have external triggers, but the feeling of fear comes from within.

Jeffers[26] introduces the idea of 'level 2' fears which have to do with the inner states of mind: '*They are not situation-oriented, they involve the ego*' and include rejection, success, failure, being conned, helplessness, disapproval and loss of image.

Level 2 fears are simply thoughts about external events, so what's causing them to turn into the physical symptoms of fear?

Regardless of which of the thousands of external fear-inducing situations you could be faced with, they all come to the same apex and the feeling that 'I just can't handle it'.

To eliminate the effect of fear on your life, you don't have to control the outside world, you simply have to develop the capacity to manage your internal state, and then trust that you have that capacity whenever it is called upon. The final chapter of this book is about self-belief, and it ties all the threads of our journey together – by having solid self-belief, you have the answer to managing fear. But let's not wait until the end. What can we get started with now to diminish the impact of fear?

Wouldn't it be cool to know that when you come across things you fear, you could sit serenely with a confident inner voice that says, 'I can handle it,' allowing your intelligent brain to focus on simply being your natural self?

It's Not as Bad as I Thought It Would Be

Fear of something will persist until you do it and reflect on it. When facing a fear, your options are:

1. Remain afraid of it forever, or
2. Step into the fear and just do it.

'@$?&!!! Where's the nice option?'

Have you ever said to yourself, 'That wasn't as bad as I thought it would be'? Of course you have. This is because your mind was having a wonderful time fantasising for hours (sometimes days, weeks, months, and years) about just how bad a catastrophe could unfold if you dared to step into the situation. The reality is never quite so bad.

Reflect & Write: What things have turned out not to be quite as bad as you imagined?

Here's an interesting statistic, over 90 per cent of what we worry about never happens[27]. As Dale Carnegie says, *'Remember, today is the tomorrow you worried about yesterday.'*

Reflect & Write: Do you have any examples of things that you used to worry about, but no longer do? If so, how did you overcome them?

'Just Do It' Evidence

What's interesting is that the more times we face a fear and push through it, the more confidence we have that we can push through the next one. There's a snowball effect. Those people who shy away from uncomfortable feelings at every turn will find more and more things to feel uncomfortable about. While those that face them head-on, and actually seek them out, find that fewer and fewer everyday things induce a sense of fear.

Reflect & Write: Let's start small. Of the tiny things that you have typically avoided, which do you plan to stop avoiding from today? List five. When the circumstance arises, just do them. Then reflect on it afterwards – was it better or worse than you feared? Did you say to yourself, '*That wasn't as bad as I thought*?' Make sure to write down your intention (rather than imagining you may do it).

Everyday Courage

Each time you tackle something uncomfortable, you draw on your reserves of courage. If you stepped into any one of the above situations, then congratulations, you deserve a pat on the back. It took courage. You may be able to identify people who show unfathomable courage. I'm currently reading *Cold* by Ranulph Fiennes, (a modern-day explorer and the first person to circumnavigate the globe pole to pole), he seems to have bottomless reserves of courage. I don't have what he has, and in comparison to Ranulph perhaps you don't perceive yourself as a courageous person.

But a technique that can help is the '5-Second Rule'[28] conceived by motivational speaker Mel Robbins (check out her TED talk 'How to Stop Screwing Yourself Over'[29]). When I have taken a decision to do something that feels challenging unless I act on it quickly, my brain finds a thousand reasons not to start. So, I apply the '5-Second Rule'. Now when I hesitate before doing something that I know I should, I count backwards 5-4-3-2-1, and then I do it. In an instant, as I say the word 'zero', I take action.

Robbins says, *'If you don't act on an instinct within that five-second window, that's it. You're not doing it.'*

Go back to your list from page 89, if overthinking is getting in your way and you're procrastinating, have a go at applying Mel's '5 Second Rule'.

Expanding Your Comfort Zone

The above exercise nudges at the boundaries of your comfort zone, making it marginally bigger, but you probably have some fears that sit well outside it – let's call these 'zone fivers'. All your fears can now be categorized depending on the scale of the anxiety that they induce.

Reflect & Write: Take one of the fears you wrote down on page 82 – now, right now, imagine doing that thing. Notice how your body reacts to the thought of it, and give it a rating: 1 – it's in my comfort zone, 2 – it's on the edge but not really a big thing to overcome, 3 – it's definitely uncomfortable, and I'm getting some noticeable physical symptoms, 4 – I can't really be rational about it, my chimp brain is taking over, 5 – it's so far from happening that it feels unreal and therefore I'm not actually too concerned about it.

With the experiment in the last section, you've begun to eat into zone 2. Remember, the fear exists until it is faced. So, what else is in your zone 2 that you're going to face? Once you've tackled these, you'll observe that zone 3 things are no longer out of reach, some of them are simply at the new edge of the comfort zone. From your list above, circle two or three which you feel you'll address next.

Just for fun, imagine that over the next year, you go on a fear-busting crusade and successfully expand your comfort zone all the way to include zone 4. You're on a roll, and next up is one of the big ones in zone 5.

Reflect & Write: Select the most exciting one. If you could face this fear and make it feel comfortable, what difference would it make to your life? If you knew you wouldn't fail, what would you attempt to do?

REFRAMING FEAR

Big Fear, Little Fear

Fear can paralyse, or it can stimulate strong determination. And you get to choose. If I were to fear a life of loneliness, I could take the victim mindset and find all the reasons why this could come true and spiral into a fear of rejection. I might avoid socializing to prevent feeling rejected, and therefore become lonelier. Or I use the fear to give me a kick up the arse. I fear the significant psychological damage caused by loneliness. I am motivated to engage in activities that feel on the edge of my comfort zone to combat it. If the fear of loneliness wasn't there, I might lack the motivation to push through short-term discomfort.

Reflect & Write: What significant long-term fear do you have, and what uncomfortable things do you need to confront in the short-term for you to feel better? What's the worst that could happen if you stepped into the little fear? (Run these questions through for five different big fears.)

Discomfort in Too Much Comfort

When things get too comfortable, they get boring. Time passes, life goes by. You are this amazing unique human being (as we established in Chapter 1), built to experience life and contribute to society. Sitting in a comfortable harbour actually induces a sense of restlessness that can feel, ironically, uncomfortable. Those feelings that dance within us when we test the edge of our comfort zone help us feel alive. Next time you sense them, be grateful.

You want to find the sweet spot between feeling totally out of control and thrown about by storms, versus lazily watching time float by, stuck in the doldrums. If you want to achieve your potential, you need to happily explore the limits, and then take action to add or remove excitement. Franklin D Roosevelt said it nicely: 'A smooth sea never made a skilled sailor.'

Is It Just Excitement?

Consider something that you would be wonderfully excited about doing. Not just a little bit, I mean super-excited. Next week I go to South Africa with my wife, and I'm so excited about the moment when we've picked up our hired 4x4 camper, got comfortable with how it drives, left the city behind us, and pulled off from a highway onto an empty gravelled country road with the sun low in the sky in the rear-view mirror, mountains in the distance, and vineyards either side.

Wow, I'm already there!

Pick your wonderfully exciting moment. What is it? Visualize it clearly in your mind or write it down if you prefer. Now allow yourself to fully experience this future moment. Imagine all the details, run it like a movie trailer, add the sounds and smells. Keep it running. Gaze gently out of the window as you daydream. Allow your imagination to carry you away.

Reflect & Write: How does it feel to visualize your fantasy moment? What sensations do you notice in your body right now?

Do you notice the similarities between the physical symptoms that we connect with the word 'excitement', and the symptoms we connect with the word 'fear'? Almost identical, right? So how about this for an audacious flip of perception: When you feel these same physical symptoms and automatically label them as 'being afraid', instead, consciously give it a new label – 'the excitement of facing something new'.

Yes, I was sceptical at first, too. Then I tried it with public speaking. I'm a professional facilitator of events, and every time before they start my pulse races, my stomach gets queasy, I go to the loo quite a lot, my palms (and armpits) sweat, I compulsively check my notes, my speech gets quicker, and my eyes dart back and forth.

When I label these symptoms as 'nerves', they get worse, and I can believe that I'm going to forget my words or go bright red. But when I started to label my symptoms as 'wide-eyed excitement' and being grateful for the adrenaline that is making me alert, then the rising symptoms become OK. Now, years later, it is with welcome relief that these feelings arise. If they ever don't come, then it's time for me to do something new as I'll be in my comfort zone and no longer bringing my 'A' game to every event.

Cock-ups

Occasionally you put off starting something important because you're worried about messing it up. You procrastinate over decisions because the over-analysis of the chimp brain has convinced you that one path leads to almost certain humiliation, pain and suffering – but you don't know which one. The easy option is to do nothing and let the outside world decide your destiny. But for you to Own Life, you've got to make the decision. In an increasingly VUCA world (volatile, uncertain, complex, ambiguous), you will have to make decisions that aren't black and white, meaning that the outcomes can't be perfectly predicted.

Remember, life is the journey, not the destination. Whatever path we choose, there will be some things that go surprisingly well, and we can be grateful for them; and some things that challenge us. Every time there is a challenge, there is an opportunity for growth. You've heard phrases like 'I've learnt more from my failures than my successes', or 'there's no such thing as failure, only feedback'. So, while a cock-up may feel bad at the time, within it lies a rich development opportunity. So be thankful and know that you'll never meet a strong person that's had an easy past.

Celebrate the troubles. And know that there is no wrong path – they either lead to great outcomes, or great lessons, or perhaps both. Sometimes the best things in life arise from moments that originally felt 'bad'.

Reflect & Write: How about you? Have you ever come through something difficult and, on reflection, consider it to be one of the best things that ever happened? What was it?

PANIC

What Is a Panic Attack?[30]

Panic attacks are a type of fear response. They're an exaggeration of the body's normal response to danger, stress or excitement. If you've never suffered from one, I've heard them described beautifully as the feeling you get

when you've rocked back on a chair slightly too far, and it's about to fall – except the pounding feeling in your chest doesn't pass quickly, and you have no idea why it started.

In anxiety attacks, you

may feel fearful, apprehensive, feel your heart racing or feel short of breath, but it's very short-lived, and when the stressor goes away, the anxiety attack dissipates. Panic attacks, on the other hand, don't come in reaction to a stressor; they're unprovoked and unpredictable.

Attacks Always Pass

Panic attacks aren't dangerous despite how they feel in the moment. You can't faint since your high heart rate is raising rather than lowering your blood pressure (the cause of passing out), and unless the intense pain in your chest literally floors you, it's not a heart attack. If there is a shortness of breath, the mix of oxygen and carbon dioxide in the bloodstream is out of proportion, which can lead to a feeling of light-headedness but can't lead to suffocation, as the breath will always, eventually, return to normal. Most panic attacks last between five and 20 minutes, with symptoms peaking within 10 minutes[31], and then they pass. Always.

If some symptoms last longer then it's likely that there is an underlying cause of anxiety, and while this chapter may help you, it may be helpful for you to seek additional support from your doctor or a counsellor.

Here are some techniques that can both stave off a panic attack and help ease one on its way if it arrives.

Breath Awareness

Place your right hand high on your chest. Place your left hand on your belly. Breathe normally and focus your attention on the movement of your hands. Set a timer on your phone and give a full minute of pure awareness to the motion without attempting to change it in any way.

How do you feel now? If you started with a calm state of

mind, it's likely that you now feel very relaxed. The internal chatter of the mind has subsided, you feel at peace and yet still alert.

The breath is always with you and has been since birth. Practising 'breath awareness' is one of the most useful techniques for maintaining balance and a sense of perspective. To survive any moment, all that is required is air in your lungs, and there it is – always, just there!

When you find anxious thoughts arising, a great habit to foster is to turn your attention to the movement of the breath for 60 seconds. And even better, make breath awareness a daily habit whether you're feeling anxious or not – the practice will make it easier when you need it most.

The fact that you have the only thing that is truly necessary for life right here is reassuring and will instantly reduce all other stress symptoms. Get into the routine of practising this when you sense the first feelings of unease, and you'll reduce the frequency of falling into the full throes of panic.

Mindfulness

Mindfulness is the psychological process of bringing your attention to experiences happening in the present moment. If your internal experiences are uncomfortable, the practice can be unhelpful as it can accentuate the feeling of discomfort, so from a stress-relieving perspective, it's important to tune into what you can experience about the external world.

Let's give this a go right now. Start by tuning into your sense of sound. Set a timer for 60 seconds, and then get comfortable. Close your eyes (to remove visual distractions), and simply notice all the sounds in your environment, ensuring that you're gathering the data from noises both near and far.

How was that?

For me, sound works best. For others, one of the other senses may be more powerful. Try a different way of seeing:

Bring both arms straight out in front of you at eye level, with your hands clenched, knuckles touching, and your thumbs sticking straight up. Close one eye and look directly through the gap between your thumbs, bringing your focus onto whatever falls within the narrow field of view.

Really concentrate on it, noticing the colour, texture, and how light falls on it. You are experiencing 'foveal vision', and it is associated with deep concentration. Now, keeping both thumbs in your field of view, and at eye level, move your hands slowly apart until they are stretched out sideways. Check that both thumbs are still in your field of view by giving them a little wiggle.

You are now experiencing something called 'peripheral vision'[32]. Lower your arms but relax the muscles around your eyes and allow everything in your field of view to be in your visual awareness. When your eyes focus or get naturally drawn to something specific, simply invite everything else back into your awareness.

Sit calmly in this state for as long as you like. Returning, when distracted, to the whole picture.

How was that? How are you feeling now? Has your breathing slowed, has your mind chatter ceased? Are you feeling calmer, yet alert? This is the effect of mindfulness, and now you know how to get into the peripheral vision you don't need to do the whole arm-raising thing, it's possible to shift your state simply by sitting with an expanded field of vision whenever you like.

A third method is to bring attention to what you are touching. No need to close your eyes this time, or raise your arms, you can do this on the train without anyone else knowing that you are doing it!

Wherever your body makes contact with something, place your attention on it. In detail! Just one touchpoint at a time and when you feel you have noticed everything there is to notice about how it physically feels, then move to touch-point number two. Once you have gone around each touchpoint, return to whichever one now calls for your attention and notice what has changed in your perception since you last gave it your full attention.

Whichever method you use, you are experiencing mindfulness, and it is proven to reduce anxiety. Like all skills, mindfulness requires practice, and it's better to practice when things aren't too difficult rather than test your novice technique in the crucible of stress. Try one technique per day. Set a time when you will do it – perhaps when you are commuting, or at the bus stop, or right before you turn on the computer. You choose how you will develop it as a positive habit.

GRIT

Dig In

IQ doesn't perfectly correlate to school grades. Research by popular science author Angela Duckworth[33] found that *'the biggest predictor of success isn't IQ, it is grit.'* It turns out that trying really hard matters too! So I was super happy when my son started primary school, and within a fortnight was enthusiastically talking about one of the school mottos (and the foundation of grit): 'We Persevere.'

Interestingly, grit isn't correlated to talent. Duckworth relates grit to the growth mindset – as we saw in Chapter 2, the ability to learn isn't fixed. For individuals with a growth mindset, failure isn't a permanent condition; they know that the brain grows in response to challenges. As you have worked through the exercises in the previous sections, you have grown your grit, and therefore statistically speaking, you are more likely to be successful than before you picked up this book. Sometimes you just have to dig in, the treasure is buried deep – perseverance is required.

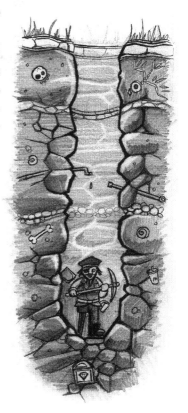

How Gritty Are You?

Head on over to AngelaDuckworth.com for a 10-question test which gives you a personal grit score, and if you don't have access to the Internet right now simply ponder this statement:

'I finish whatever I begin.'

The degree to which you agree with the statement is likely to be similar to the degree to which you have grit.

Low grit ratings mean that you've got space to grow and can expect greater success if you're willing to bring a growth mindset to them.

The next chapter tackles everything to do with setting

powerful goals that keep you motivated and focussed on the long term. Before we get there though, how do you feel about setbacks?

Bounce-back-ability

When you simply see results, it may appear that success comes easily to some people. But the reality is that on most occasions when you look more deeply, the difference between success and failure is sheer persistence.

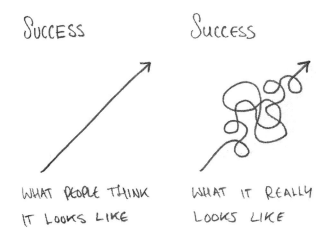

SUCCESS   SUCCESS

WHAT PEOPLE THINK IT LOOKS LIKE   WHAT IT REALLY LOOKS LIKE

Reflect & Write: Reflecting on your life, what success have you really had to work for? Select a project, something that took some time, went through some ups and downs, and that you are genuinely proud of. Draw the axis of a graph with time on the x-axis and difficulty on the y-axis. Now plot your project along the timeline – noticing the ups and downs of how it felt along the way.

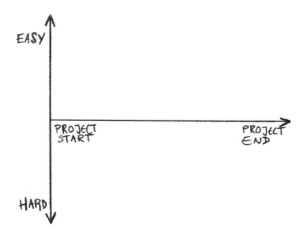

When you hit a trough, and things got tough, how did you keep going? If your project fits almost entirely below the line – and was pretty much hard from start to finish, then how did you keep going? Why didn't you quit?

Reflect & Write: When things got tough, how did you keep going?

This project you've plotted is something that you are really proud of. On reflection, it's one of your life highlights. If it had been easy all the time, would you be as proud? Would it have been a life highlight? If you didn't have to push through challenges, would you be genuinely proud of anything?

Everything you do that matters will have ups and downs, and sometimes the 'ups' only come after the project ends and you can reflect with pride about how you overcame the 'downs'. How much you are prepared to suffer to achieve the goal depends on how much you care about the outcome.

When setting goals in the next chapter, we'll make sure that they really do matter. To achieve your goal, you will suffer. This is essential for growth, and for the deep sense of achievement that comes when you hit the finish line.

Giving Up vs Letting Go

If I give up it means I'm throwing in the towel of defeat, my perseverance is gone, and I am disappointed. This is entirely different from those things I choose to let go of. Letting go means I free myself from something that is not important enough to continue striving for.

In the past, you may have given yourself a hard time for quitting something when, in reality, you were freeing yourself. At one time, I would always finish a book that I started reading; until I acknowledged that some books weren't worth the effort. I freed myself, and now I read more good books because I am happy to let go of the bad ones. If you're carrying unhelpful baggage, then to fly, you have to throw it overboard. The bags that you throw out, if you choose them carefully, aren't important to your life success but they are holding you back. So, let them go. They are not failures, but they may be causing your life to fail.

Reflect & Write: It's probably also true that sometimes you gave up because you lacked grit. Let's get examples of each: Write down five challenges that you were right to let go of, and then five challenges that you gave up.

It may now feel better to re-label some things as 'letting go', and this is critical to achieving the big stuff (we'll return to this topic when we look at time management in Chapter 6).

Reflect & Write: When you look at the other list, the list of things that you gave up on, how does it feel?

Reflect & Write: Reflecting on the five (or more) scenarios where you've given up, list all the reasons why, in the past, you have quit.

Applying a Growth Mindset

Run through the list and see where accountability lies. If other more important priorities came along then it's not 'quitting', it is 'letting go', and is good prioritization, so you can cross those off the list. If you've written something that is within your control (e.g. procrastination, fear of failure, etc.) then great, we'll take action on those things next. If something on your list is due to something entirely outside your sphere of control (e.g. legislation change made it illegal), then you can write those off as 'shit happens', the world isn't fair.

But if you regularly seem to say, 'Why does it always happen to me?' then check whether you are taking appropriate accountability for your own life or looking externally to divert blame. Take a look at anything on your list that isn't entirely in your control, but you could have influence over (e.g. teammates). If you wrote, 'I quit because my boss doesn't like me', or 'my teammate didn't pull their weight', then you are externalising all the blame, and this won't help you in the future when facing similar challenges. So, rewrite anything where you have influence so that you can then choose a course of action. For example, 'I quit because I was unable to manage my emotional responses towards certain behaviours of my boss', or 'I quit because I wasn't able to inspire and motivate my teammates effectively'. The rewording may feel subtle but it fundamentally shifts your position from victim to empowered.

Taking what you know about the growth mindset from Chapter 2, in the past, these things have caused you to quit. But they don't have to in the future because the brain grows through challenge. You can be more capable of pushing through the challenges in the future, so let's put a 'yet' into a sentence and then you can give yourself some advice for the future.

Here's an example:
I quit because other team members weren't pulling their weight. I'm not able to motivate lazy people... yet. When an important goal is blocked by lazy people in the future, the advice I have for myself is to: a) find the right words to be gently straight with them about how I feel about their work ethic, and/or b) try to find out what is getting in their way and therefore stand in their shoes a little better; and/or c) reallocate the work and take the person off the project; and/or d) accept that I have to step in more (suck it up because the world isn't fair).

Reflect & Write: Over to you, take three of the most common reasons why you have quit in the past. Write it as a growth mindset statement (i.e. it includes the word 'yet'), and then give yourself some advice for the future.

Perfectionism

I sometimes hear people say, 'I'm a perfectionist', and they're guiltily proud of this trait. But little gets in the way of happiness or progress more than an expectation of perfection. It's a common reason to quit something. But we don't have to ditch the quest for perfection, we simply need to reframe the level at which it is applied. When it's applied at the micro-level, where every little thing needs to be perfectly completed, then it's stifling and causes the big picture to be a million miles from perfection.

So, we need to flip things. What we really seek is the perfect big picture, which means accepting that everything within the picture has to be good enough.

For example, when I visualize my perfect life it includes authoring best-selling self-help books; facilitating large training events; training for endurance sports events; being very present in my kids' everyday lives; long frequent conversations with my wife; and travelling the world. Each element needs to be present in the big picture, and each needs to be 'right-sized' to allow space for all the other elements to fit.

At this level, it's now easy to see that perfection actually means 'the right size for the total composition', and not 'maximized'. In practice, this means that my sports training is 'right-sized' to get me to the start and finish line of endurance events, but not onto the podium, since training to that level would squash all the other elements and make the big picture pretty ugly.

At a micro-level, I could be self-critical that I'm not achieving my sporting potential, yet by stepping back and seeing the entirety of life, I can see that I am achieving my life potential. You sometimes have to let go of damaging expectations in one area to paint the full picture.

What has this got to do with resilience? It's about expectation setting. Too many of us give ourselves a hard time because we're not living up to our imagination of what perfection looks like, and so we quit.

Reflect & Write. How about you? In what areas of your life are you setting yourself an unrealistically high expectation?

Reframing Failure

People with a fixed mindset see success or failure as evidence that someone is talented or not, and therefore failure should be avoided. This causes them to take the safe options, stay in the comfort zone, and feel good about repeatedly doing the same things well. They are stuck. To grow means putting yourself into new situations where, by definition, you have less experience. Measured against those things you have already mastered, the new things you try will feel awkward, and great results will be less easy to come by. Measured in this way, failure is inevitable. The growth mindset celebrates effort above talent. Failure is simply feedback.

Here's a nice way to reframe the goal of any activity so that you are guaranteed to be 100 per cent successful all of the time: *Whatever you are doing, the goal is to learn as much as possible so that the next time you do it, you do it better.*

If the activity achieves the desired outcome, what did you do that made it successful? And what could you do to make it more successful? If it failed, what have you learnt that would increase the chance of success next time?

Reflect & Write. Consider something that you failed at

recently. What have you learnt about yourself, others, or the environment?

There genuinely is no such thing as failure as long as you have a growth mindset, so when facing challenges, set yourself the goal to learn.

Habits for Success

There's no single silver bullet that leads to success; it's a meandering path of failure, lessons and grit. It takes a suite of skills that need practice. The techniques are all in this book; it's up to you to put them into action. What would make you more resilient to setbacks so that you'll keep digging?

(Here's a list, which is very similar to the list of contents for this book):

- Believing that I'm fine just the way I am. (Chapter 1)
- Accepting that I can change and adopting a growth mindset. (Chapter 2)
- Acknowledging and managing shifting emotions. (Chapter 3)
- Handling setbacks and inner critic. (Chapter 4)
- A strong sense of purpose, razor-sharp goals and good planning. (Chapter 5)
- Taking care of the most precious commodity, time. (Chapter 6)
- Maintaining positive mental, physical and emotional energy. (Chapter 7)
- Nurturing a caring support network. (Chapter 8)
- Believing in myself. (Chapter 10)

Concluding Thoughts

Fear is a natural human instinct that keeps you safe. However, sometimes its overprotective nature holds you back. By acknowledging the fear, and consistently facing into gently increasing doses of it, you develop a greater capacity to quieten the limiting beliefs that you hold and begin to say hello to the voice that says, 'I can handle anything.'

The journey to success isn't a straight line, you will have setbacks. By combining grit with a growth mindset, failure can be turned into a rich lesson that brings you closer to your goals.

When El Davo first draws an illustration, he's super disappointed. He's not an accomplished speed-drawer (yet!). In his pencil case, he carries five different kinds of erasers and describes them as his favourite tool as they release him from the need for perfection. His bin overflows with failures, yet it's his grit and growth mindset that turns each one into a lesson and allows him to produce stunning art.

CHAPTER 5
MAKING DREAMS
COME TRUE

Only Cinderella has a fairy godmother, the rest of us have to rely on ourselves. But we don't need a magic wand; we simply need to know the secret formula. That's what this chapter is about: the formula to turn dreams into reality. So, go on, dream big and let's really make the most of this precious lifetime.

GOAL HUNTING

What do you want? It's a straightforward question. Your initial reaction could range from 'nothing at all', to 'what don't I!', or perhaps you swing from one end of the spectrum to the other depending on your philosophical mood. Do you want to be healthy? Yes. So that's one. Let's get a full picture of everything that you want.

> **Reflect & Write:** Some things may already be popping up for you, so let's just capture what's in your head right now. If nothing is coming up, then that's fine too, as you can use the next few sections to give some structure to find your goals. Finish the following sentence over and over until you run out of things to write: *I want...*

Bucket List

To 'kick the bucket' is an 18th Century British phrase meaning 'to die', and a 'bucket list' has become associated with a list of all the activities that someone wants to do before they die.

> **Reflect & Write:** Remembering YOLO (you only live once), so dream big. Write down 10 things that are on your bucket list.

The Wheel of Life

After having just taken a very long-term perspective, we'll now use the wheel of life to look at things in the round. The wheel represents life and is divided into eight important aspects of life.

> **Reflect & Write.** For each aspect of the wheel of life, ask yourself the question, 'How satisfied am I right now?' Copy out this wheel in your notebook or journal. Mark your score

on the wheel and then colour in the segment (0 is complete dissatisfaction, and 10 is complete satisfaction). Use the space around the wheel to makes some notes about why you scored it the way you did.

PS – it's better if I don't give you my definition for each segment because then it would come through my filters and not yours. Whatever a word means to you is the right definition.

If you've rated every section 10, then you'd be the first that I've come across. It's more likely that you have a gap between where you are now and complete satisfaction. And it's OK to leave things exactly as they are. Or, if you would like greater life satisfaction, it is useful to set some goals around each segment you wish to improve.

Reflect & Write: In a single sentence, capture your goal for one segment. Then repeat it for as many sections as you'd like to improve.

Reflect & Write: What's missing from the lists you've created in this chapter? There's always something that doesn't fit neatly into one of the categories. What additional goals do you have?

More will come up over time, and when they do, add them to your page. But perhaps now you realize quite how much you want to achieve. Now you have recorded your goals you can objectively do something with them.

PRIORITIZATION
The Busy Fool
Count the total number of goals that you now realize that you have in life. How many do you have?

If you started the planning process for each one of them simultaneously, what would happen? Either you'd begin doing stuff without a robust plan, and then get frustrated when things quickly go off the rails, or you'd spend years furiously spinning plates that begin to wobble if they don't get enough attention, and occasionally breaking the most important one.

You are likely to already be busy, but are you a busy fool? Clocking up the hours of work, ticking off your to-do list, but in reality, going around in circles. The next chapter looks at *how* you can use your time effectively, here we'll be looking at *what* you want to do with your time. We'll take the total number of goals you have and identify your top five priorities.

Clustering

Imagine that each of your goals is written on its own sticky note. You can now, metaphorically, stick each one to a wall – putting the ones that are similar close to each other – so you end up with several clusters (and a few odd ones that don't neatly fit into a cluster). Each cluster will have a theme – a single overarching goal that encompasses all the sticky notes that fall within it. Working at the overarching goal level raises the stakes and should be more impactful. But don't lose the individual stickies because they may form your stepping stones.

Reflect & Write: Have a go at consolidating any individual goals that seem to fit together snugly in natural clusters. Don't force it too much. If you do, the individual clusters can get too busy, and you end up with a single overarching goal that says something like 'be happy' (which is then difficult to plan).

You now have a handful of goal areas with some supporting thoughts about what they include. You also have the individual goals that don't fit into a cluster. That doesn't mean they are less important, it simply means that you wrote it down once, and once was enough. So what?

Reflect & Write: Imagine you can be successful at any one of the goals you now have. What would be the impact? Write your long list of goals down the left-hand side of a page, then for each one, capture what the benefit is in a second column. Finally, ask yourself, *So what?* If your internal gut response is 'blah' then score it low (0), if your insides are dancing about or you're feeling mildly sick, then score it high (10). Write your scores for each goal in a third column.

Your North Star

The entire northern sky wheels around the North Star and for many centuries explorers have used it to guide them when local landmarks are unavailable. Having a single guiding mission is sometimes useful when making decisions about what to prioritize. Just as explorers never intended to actually travel to the North Star (they simply used it as a way to set their bearings); the same can be true for your guiding star.

My guiding star is to 'grow the world's emotional intelligence', my friend Nigel's is 'to enable people to live with greater grace and flow', and another friend Jefferson's is 'to establish a fearless culture'. Some famous ones are Mark Zuckerberg, 'to connect the world'; Gary Vaynerchuck, 'to own the New York Jets'; and back in 1995 Jeff Bezos wrote 'to build earth's most customer-centric company'.

Snappy sentences like the ones above take time to craft.

They sometimes bubble up out of nowhere, and sometimes it's like tapping the shell of a walnut over and over until the nut inside is finally revealed. For now, you can release any pressure of pinpointing an actual North Star, simply pointing Northwards is good enough. You can probably sense what it isn't (your southerly direction), so let's get these down first.

Reflect & Write: Complete this sentence multiple times: *My guiding North Star is definitely NOT...*

That might have felt quite easy. How about what may be to your east or west? These are things that aren't directly opposite to where you want to head in life, but also, they don't feel like they are directly in your forward path either. You can be happy to let them go in this lifetime.

Reflect & Write: Complete this sentence multiple times: *As I walk my life, I am happy to pass by...*

So, we're now looking forwards, what is in your field of view? What would you like to write down that could help to act as a beacon through your life? Anything that arises is absolutely fine.

Reflect & Write: Complete the following statement: *I can use the following thoughts to guide my path into the future...*

When you close this book and go to do something different, your subconscious mind will go to work on the question. Sometimes it will produce amazingly different and insightful results. So, add to and amend your lists over time.

Here, I'll pause briefly. There is no pressure to fill it at all.

But if you do have a snappy sentence that could act as your North Star note it down.

You now have another method of rating the relative importance of your long list of goals: How close to your true north do they take you? On page 117, you have a list of potential goals with 'so what' scores, highlight any that are lined up with your North Star.

Prioritization Axis

You can now rank the relative importance of each of your goals with those that get both a high 'so what' score are highlighted, ranking most highly. Go back to the list and rank them, with a number 1 being the most important. Use this as your Y-axis.

Now consider how challenging each one might be to accomplish. Each will be challenging in different ways: some requiring dedicated time; some requiring you to overcome fear; some needing stamina and perseverance. To rank them, consider how much energy it would take you to really go after this goal for the next six months. A rating of a 10 would be equivalent to you sprinting non-stop for six months, a 5 is sustained breathlessness, and a 1 is a gentle jog. (Note: I'm using exercise as a metaphor, learning French wouldn't leave me physically breathless but it would still be tiring.) Go back to your list of goals, squeeze an additional column on your page, title it 'energy required' and then rate each goal. This is your X-axis.

Reflect & Write: Recreate the graph below in your notebook and plot each goal onto it

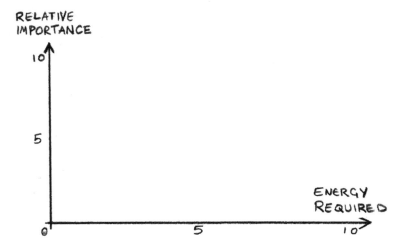

What could this graph show you? If you drew a 'best-fit' line through your points and it slopes from top left to bottom right, this means that the more important your goals are to you, the more effort is required for you to achieve them. This equation is nicely balanced: Effort = Reward. You could choose any of these as goals.

For any goals that sit above this diagonal line, the effort required is greater than the relative reward and this naturally leads to a significant self-motivation challenge. Would you really see it through to the end? Would the end result be sufficiently satisfying? These goals are the prime candidates for being dropped.

The real gold lies underneath the diagonal line. If you have any goals that sit in the bottom left corner of your graph, then these are your priorities as they take little energy for relatively large-scale rewards.

Priority Goals

Over the past few sections, you've been using your logical left brain to bring some rigour to your choice of priority goals. It's now time to allow the logic to sit in the background and acknowledge the power of gut feeling in the final decision-making process.

Of your list of goals, which ones are now calling to you? Select five that you feel most motivated about, and we'll work on sharpening them in the next section. For the remainder, they remain on the reserve list, ready to be picked up in the future; or not. The key to achieving your goals is to bring focus to the most important ones (rather than half-doing lots and lots).

Reflect & Write: Write down your five top-priority goals.

'HELL YEAH' GOALS
Begin with the End in Mind
'Imagination is everything. It is the preview of life's coming attractions', said Einstein, and we can use this preview to bring clarity to any goal. You now have five prioritized goal areas. Taking each one in turn, (assuming that you have the right strategy, and work hard, and luck is on your side), choose a specific moment in the future when you'll know that this goal has been achieved. Close your eyes, take yourself to this future moment.

Reflect & Write: What is happening in your imagination? Let your mind wander, see all the details, add all the sounds. When you have a clear picture for each goal, write down a sentence that defines success for you. Now add a date to that specific moment. When can you allow yourself to believe that this event could happen? Be absolutely specific. 'Next year' isn't precise enough. Pick a date. If you write 'ongoing', then seek to identify a future moment when you can imagine hitting a noticeable milestone.

Does It Tingle?
When you close your eyes and imagine the moment of success, does it tingle? Look back to page 94 where you wrote how your fantasy excitement moment feels. Do you feel the same now about achieving your goal? If not, then the goal lacks excitement, and you're guaranteed to lack motivation. Just bringing your goal into your mind should bring butterflies to your stomach. If you don't yet get a tingle for all five of your goals, you will soon, just keep on reading.

Specificity

If a goal is too generic (i.e. it is the same as a lot of other people would write), it is harder for you personally to get attached to it. A generic goal may be: 'a job I enjoy', and the moment you know you've achieved success is when you are 'looking forward to the alarm going off on a Monday morning'. If we were in a personal coaching session, I would next ask you, 'Tell me more about the imaginary job that you enjoy so much.' If your current goal is a little too generic, ask yourself a 'tell me more' question, and build some details into your goal statement.

Stretching Without Breaking

If the goal is too easy, then there's no buzz. Is there a reason why you're limiting your ambition? Could you allow yourself to want twice as much, or achieve the goal twice as fast? An exciting goal has to have a significant stretch. Imagine pulling an elastic band as wide as it will go – are you really operating right at the extremes? If you pull the band one per cent more then it snaps. If you believe that you've stretched the goal beyond its breaking point, then you need to back off a little, otherwise you'll mentally give up before you start.

Being able to learn sufficient French to ask for a croissant during our family trip next year won't stretch me. Delivering next week's event in Paris in French is out of the question. Learning sufficient French to give a two-minute introduction to the guest speaker before next week is potentially possible, and the thought of it is now giving me butterflies (bingo! That's what we're looking for!).

Too Near or Too Far?

If something feels like it's over the horizon, even if there's time to make the journey, it can lack a realness that comes with being able to feel the progress. Before I die, I want to have enhanced the emotional intelligence of the UK population. I can see what success looks like, and I can put an estimated date on it. But it's hard for me to feel the tingle of excitement because the end result just feels too distant. If your goal feels like it's over the horizon, then we need to bring it closer. In half the time, what would success look like? And if you halved the timescale again, what is your new definition of success?

In my case, 30 years becomes 15, which becomes seven years. What does success look like to me seven years from now? A quarter of all UK university undergraduates receive emotional intelligence training alongside their academic training which results in a 10 per cent rise in their EQ (emotional quotient).

Ooooooo, that feels better!

Conversely, a quick-win goal is motivating, but if that marks the end of the road, then the motivation is wasted. If this is the case for you, then consider your current goal as being an important stepping-stone towards something bigger. Giving a two-minute introduction in French next week will make me feel great. But what if it leads onwards into the future, step-by-step, towards giving a 10-minute keynote talk in French in 12 months? The great feeling of next week becomes a motivator for a much grander goal.

Are your goals pitched right? If you scaled them up or down, do they become more or less motivating? Take a look at each one in turn and refine them.

Connecting with 'Why'

When you were selecting your five priority goals, you put each of them through a brief 'so what' question. Now that you have the 'focus five' let's get into the heart of why they are so important to you. (You have seen this series of questions before, on page 20.)

Reflect & Write: For each goal, in turn, write down why it is important to you. Once you've done that, challenge yourself to be honest, and complete this sentence: *That REALLY matters to me because...*

When you craft your final goal sentence, put a 'because' in it, and find a snappy way to articulate why it really matters to you: *'I want university students to have higher EQ because it directly correlates with happy, successful lives'*.

Doubt: The Tingle Suppressant

If your goal really matters and could significantly improve your life, is tangible enough for you to picture what success looks like and it is at the limit of your potential but not beyond it, then you will have butterflies of excitement. If you don't feel them it is because they are masked by other emotions, but trust me, they are there.

Self-doubt is the biggest tingle suppressant. You may accept that, in theory, you have the potential to achieve these things, but you have low confidence that you actually will. We dealt with the fear of failure in the last chapter, and later on we'll look at the causes of failure and how to overcome the most common ones (time, energy, other people, and self-doubt).

Also, remember how closely related the physical sensations of excitement and fear are (page 94). My daughter has a word to describe how she feels before performing on stage, 'nerv-excited', and it's the best description of how I feel when reading an awesome goal sentence.

EXACTly

We've been looking at ways to make goals more motivating, and in a moment I'd like you to have a go at crafting awesome goal sentences. You may have come across the acronym SMART concerning setting goals, which in my view is great for rational corporate objectives but lacks the inner burst of energy required to be motivating for individuals. If you haven't come across SMART, don't worry, we're going to use something better. When I did my initial coach training, I was introduced to the EXACT[34] model for goal setting, developed by the inspiring Carol Wilson and taught to me by the wise James Mackenzie Wright.

EXACT is a simple acronym that brings together all the concepts considered in this section. Use it as a checklist when crafting each of your goals.

> E = **Explicit:** Succinct, precise and with one focus.
> X = **eXciting:** Inspiring, motivating, and connected with a deeper 'why'.
> A = **Assessable:** Measurable, you know when you've achieved it.
> C = **Challenging:** Stretching to 'almost breaking point'.
> T = **Time framed:** Three to six months (not over the horizon, and not tomorrow).

Crafting Goals

At the start of this section, you drafted some goal areas and considered what success would look like, now we will pause again to ensure that they are crafted with real care. In the words of Stephen Covey, *'It's incredibly easy to get caught up in an activity trap, in the busyness of life, to work harder and harder climbing the ladder of success only to discover it's leaning against the wrong wall.'*[35]

For the rest of this chapter we'll get busy climbing the ladder, so first, let's get 'EXACTly' clear which wall it is that you want to be climbing.

Reflect & Write: Write down your five EXACT goals in succinct sentences on a fresh piece of paper.

FINDING THE PATH

Now you're clear on your destination, what route will you take to get there? Will you take the same path you've tried before, follow in the footsteps of others, or plough your own furrow? We'll use a creative thinking technique to help you see all the possibilities, and the GROW model to help you on your way.

The GROW Model

Developed by Sir John Whitmore in the 1980s and made popular in his book *Coaching for Performance*[36], the GROW model is one of the most widely used models in corporate coaching. We'll work through the four stages of the model to help you to find your path:

G = Goal: What do you want?
R = Reality: Where are you now?
O = Options: What could you do?
W = Will: What will you do?

The most important of the steps is the goal, because you need to make sure that your ladder is leaning up against the right wall. You have some EXACT goals, so the first step is done. Let's get into the rest.

You have already given some thought to what success looks like for each of your goals. Consider this to be your 10/10 perfect result. Now we'll assess the Reality of your current position.

Reflect & Write: Contemplate where you are right now. What score would you give yourself for each of your five EXACT goals and why? (0 is 'I have no relevant experience, and I have no idea how to start'. Anything 7 or above is 'I have learnt lots from my past and have a solid strategy for reaching my goal'.) Jot some notes next to the scores so that you have a reminder of your rationale.

Creative Thinking to increase Options

In the creative process, there are two modes of thinking, divergent and convergent, yet we typically attempt to shortcut the process by doing them concurrently.

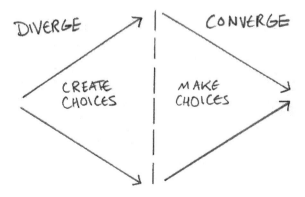

When we're efficient, we have an idea and then instantly judge it as good or bad. This leads us to repeatedly execute the same strategies. Often credited to Einstein, *'The definition of insanity is doing the same thing over and*

over again but expecting different results'. By separating the two ways of thinking, we can generate innovative solutions.

In the 'divergent thinking' phase, we diverge from a question to establish the widest possible spread of options – as required in the 'Options' step of the GROW model. Later, in the 'Will' step, you will bring judgement to the options and use 'convergent thinking' to decide what you will do.

What Could You Do?

Reflect & Write: It's time to play! You're not making a commitment to do anything. Our simple objective is to get a long list of options, ranging from the sensible to the ridiculous. Fill two pages of your notebook with your creativity. For each of your goals, ask yourself: *In what ways could someone move from the 'present reality' towards the goal?*

Notice that the question says 'someone' rather than 'you' because you don't want to be constrained by your particular social conditioning, which may bring limiting filters to your creativity. Log everything that comes up, just let the pen flow. When the ideas begin to slow down, ask yourself, 'What would someone else do? What would a child do? What would the most confident version of myself do? What would an extreme extrovert do? What would a courageous person do? What would a methodical person do?' Keep asking yourself, '… and what else?'

When the ideas stop, take a break. Relax. Go to sleep. Exercise. Do something completely different. When the brain is at rest, the subconscious makes new connections, so don't force the answers. When it comes to creativity, resting is often the best strategy. I'll see you in a few days ;-)

What Will You Do?

We're into the final GROW step, and it's planning time. Considering the full range of options for each EXACT goal, which ones are you drawn to? There may be three to five strategies that feel right. They may build into a logical sequence, or they may be better suited to work in parallel.

Reflect & Write: For each goal write your plan down in a logical order. Then determine what the very first step in each journey is and precisely when you intend to do it.

CELEBRATE

Tracking Progress

When you crafted your EXACT goal statement, you ensured that it was 'Assessable', so how will you measure progress in practice? For each goal, you have a 'present reality' score. To add a point to the score requires some action, which delivers some result. Without knowing the precise actions for every step, you can still begin to imagine what would cause to you to score the 'present reality' differently.

Some are straightforward. On my bucket list is to complete an Ironman Triathlon. This is over-the-horizon, so my EXACT goal is to complete a half-Ironman in July next year in less than six hours. I attempted it last year and learnt lots about how to train effectively, so feel my present reality is a 6. Getting to 7 means, I'm consistently training for six hours per week and ready to start the prescribed Ironman fitness programme. An 8 requires sticking to the eight-week 'base-building' phase of the plan, and a 9 requires me to stick to the 'peak-performance' training for eight weeks. When I cross the line, I hit my 10!

Others need a little more lateral thinking, but I'm yet to come across a journey that can't be measured. For example, if your goal is to be confident presenting in front of a large audience, it may be difficult to put a measure on how confident you feel (as it can swing from one day to the next). So instead measure the steps which you anticipate will bring you confidence. A 2 may be 'speaking up at the next team meeting'; a 4 maybe 'giving an informal update on a project'; a 6, 'presenting a team update using Powerpoint and receiving feedback'; an 8, 'presenting updates at weekly team meetings'; and a 10, 'reflecting on my first presentation to the department'. In this example, we are measuring the inputs rather than the outcomes and assume that the two are correlated.

Reflect & Write: Applying the old saying: 'what gets measured, gets done', taking each goal in turn, how will you measure your progress?

Rewards

Your goals give you a tingle of excitement, but this isn't enough to get you through the tough times. Remember, the goals are set right at the limit of achievability, and therefore require you to be at your best – all of the time!

Sometimes you'll have off-days, even off-months. You'll notice these and feel guilty. You may be good at patting yourself on the back when you've persevered, but most people are not. It's important to build rewards into fixed milestones on your journey. The reward itself should be something tangible, but it can be small and doesn't have to relate to your goal. The real purpose of the reward is to cause you to stop, reflect, and be proud of your effort.

Reflect & Write: Complete this sentence: *The little treats I'll enjoy along the way are...*

Reward Effort, Nothing Else

If you try really hard but fail to achieve a milestone, do you deserve a reward? In the corporate world, bonuses come directly from the financial performance of the company, so it naturally follows that personal rewards are linked to achieving company objectives. But you don't have this constraint with personal goals (as long as your treat isn't something too expensive!). What we are going to reward is black and white. We reward effort. If you tried your best, you get the treat irrespective of whether the results were positive or not.

Remember the lessons from the growth mindset and the 10,000 hours of practice: if you persevere, you will be successful. So, the only thing you have to do is persevere, and the only thing we reward is perseverance.

THE POTENTIAL GAP
Forecasting Performance

If your goals are perfectly challenging, then you have the potential to achieve them. Just!

Reflect & Write: How confident are you that you will achieve them? Rate each one from 0 ('I've already quit'), to 10 ('It's a certainty').

Unless you have a series of 10's, then you are uncertain that you will achieve the goals despite having the potential. This is, of course, normal; things get in the way of performance. Yet the majority are predictable, and therefore we can do something about them before they knock us off course.

Reflect & Write: What is likely to get in your way of perfect performance? These are the potential 'derailers' (the things that could cause you to go off the rails). Considering each goal in turn, complete this sentence: *The gap between my actual performance and my potential could be caused by...*

Internal vs External

As a novice tennis coach Tim Gallwey taught the traditional techniques to his players but noticed far more impressive results when he began, instead, to focus on what was going on inside a player's mind. From this discovery came his best-selling first book, *The Inner Game of Tennis*.[37]

He then achieved success using the same technique across such diverse fields as golf, skiing, music and work; and has played a significant role in bringing the coaching profession from the sports field into corporate life. At the core of his work are three ideas:

1. Performance = Potential – Interference
2. Interference can be categorized as internal or external
3. It is the internal interferences that have the most significant impact on performance

Take a look at your list of derailers and categorize each one as either 'I' (internal) or 'E' (external). Internal ones arise from within you (for example, confidence, lack of focus, procrastination) and you are responsible for them. External ones you can't control as they are influenced by other people or the environment (for example, competition, weather, other team members). How many of each do you have?

Some are hard to pin down as one or the other. For example, 'money'. You can earn cash and prioritize your spending (internal), and you may or may not have funding sources such as parents (external). Health is another grey area. Through positive habits you can give yourself an increased chance of good health (internal), yet despite what you do, you may suffer from ill-health (external).

If Only...

Looking down the list of external interferences, put the words 'If only' in front of each one. *If only my teammates pulled their weight, then I would achieve my goals.*

When you prefix a sentence with 'if only', you are creating a fantasy world that only exists in your head; yet you need to operate in the real world. Some of the external interferences are simply a fact of an unfair life. That's the way it is, so your plans need to deal with them.

Reflect & Write: Selecting three external interferences that you have no influence over, how will you overcome them to stay on track?

Accepting Responsibility

You can't control the items on your external list, and for some, you also have no influence (such as the weather), yet for a large number, you do have a degree of influence. You now have a choice. Leave those items as external and accept their negative consequences on your future; or bring them into your sphere of influence, accept responsibility, and stay in the driving seat of your happiness.

You can influence the performance of others, or the priorities of your boss, or the impact of doubters. While you can't control a negative reality when it occurs, you can take steps to overcome a 'victim mentality'. You are not a puppet whose life is pulled this way and that by the external world –

it's time to cut the strings that have been holding you back.

Reflect & Write: Select three external interferences where you can grow your influence. Choose what actions you could now take.

The Inner Game

Reducing the impact of external interferences is a small step to increasing your confidence. The bigger step comes through the management of your inner game; your internal interferences.

There are common ones:

1. I don't have the skills necessary: see Chapter 2 on the growth mindset, what are you choosing to invest time in to get better at?
2. I lack self-belief – see Chapter 3.
3. Fear holds me back – see Chapter 4.
4. I don't have time – see Chapter 6.
5. I lack motivation – see pages 122 – 128 of this chapter.
6. I get distracted – see page 121 of this chapter to be clear on your priorities.
7. I lack energy – see Chapter 7.
8. Other people affect me – see Chapter 8.

This book is designed to help you to build a strong inner game. Keep doing the exercises, and you will be closer to achieving your potential.

What would your critical inner voice be saying to you? Imagine you're riding a bus down pleasant avenue allowing your mind to wander to a challenge that you are facing. Which voice chirps up first? Is it one of doubt? If so, what does it sound like – angry, dismissive, sneering, anxious – and what words does it say to you?

Reflect & Write: Complete this sentence: *My voice of doubt sounds like... and says...*

Now imagine inviting that voice to take a seat at the back of the bus. You can watch it shuffle off in your rear-view mirror. With that voice gone, there is silence and space. Into that silence walks a new character – your sage, your cheerleader, your biggest fan, your monk. What do they sound like, and what do they say?

Reflect & Write: Complete this sentence: *The voice of my inner cheerleader sounds like... and says...*

Of course, you are neither of these voices, in reality, you are the listener, and you can choose which voice you pay attention to.[38]

HANDLING SETBACKS

Oprah Winfrey – often ranked as the most influential woman in the world – has been chatting to successful people on her show for decades. Each one has the same piece of advice for their younger selves, 'Relax, it's going to be OK.'

Inevitable Plan Failure

When any business forecasts its monthly sales figures for the coming year, the single guarantee is that the forecast will be wrong. If a forecast is updated throughout the month, then by the end of that month they can expect a pretty accurate figure. The margin of error grows the further into the future they are trying to predict. The forecast is based on a set of assumptions, which in turn, are built from data that is available at the time they are made. Assumptions require human judgement (which we know is influenced by our unique filters), the data available is incomplete, and the world is constantly changing. Therefore version 1 of a plan that is then blindly executed will inevitably fail.

This is true for your plan too – version 1 is likely to fail. 'The Plan' isn't set in stone and must evolve as you receive new information and need to update your assumptions. This doesn't mean, however, that plans are useless and that a 'winging-it' strategy is better. A strong plan enables you to track progress, learn lessons, course correct and create plan version 2, and 3, and 4... All the way to the final plan that sees you over the finish line.

We can label a setback as a 'failure', but I like to think of them as the essential ingredient to learning what assumptions need to be updated. '*I have not failed. I've just found 10,000 ways that won't work,*' said lightbulb inventor Thomas Edison. While we don't want to replan 10,000 times, during this section we will look at how you use inevitable 'failure' to your benefit and remind ourselves of the wisdom of Henry Ford, who said, *'The only real mistake is the one from which we learn nothing.'*

Getting to the Root

When things begin to go off track, you need to identify which assumption was incorrect, update it, and then replan. For each goal you have established how you will track progress – choosing when to pause and reflect on progress is an essential ingredient in the plan. And I mean really pausing, not just being aware of an occasional nagging thought that says, 'Things aren't going well,' which you try to push away.

When you pause, the idea is to reflect on what you know now that you didn't know when you made the plan. It may be something you couldn't have known about (a freak weather storm), or something you didn't factor in (such as the competing priorities of your boss). In the second scenario, don't be hard on yourself – 'hindsight is an exact science' – it's easy to look back and think 'I should have...' and then bring harsh self-judgement. There really is no benefit to this train of thought, so let's direct the brainpower to find out what you have learnt.

Getting forensic, which specific part of the plan isn't going to plan? It's unlikely to be everything. Even if things feel like they are completely unravelling it can probably be traced back to a single root cause. The root cause can be found in one of the following categories:

1. The goal isn't a priority – it lacks a powerfully strong 'why'
2. The goal isn't appropriately challenging – it's either too easy or so stretching that it is unrealistic
3. The plan isn't robust – a lack of attention to detail when

considering the steps
4. A new or stronger external interference has emerged
5. A new or stronger internal interference has emerged

Lessons from the Past
You have been through a lot to arrive at this moment; life is littered with setbacks from which you can learn. By reflecting on the past, you can make better assumptions about the future.

Here are a few of mine:
Reflection: I didn't stick to my plan to practice the guitar every day for at least 10 minutes. Root cause: Other things filled my time. Incorrect assumption: Learning the guitar is important to me. What I've learnt: I need to know my priorities, focus on them, and let everything else go.

Reflection: I didn't get to the start line of a half-Ironman last year. Root cause: Compressing my training programme due to overseas work commitments led to injuries. Incorrect assumption: Missing a week of training can be caught up the following week. What I've learnt: Plan a training programme that works even when I am away from home.

Reflection: The first draft of illustrations for the first chapter of this book were uninspiring. Root cause: I gave too precise descriptions of what I wanted and gave no space for El Davo (the illustrator) to bring his creative talents to the table. Incorrect assumption: Having a precise brief always leads to good results. What I've learnt: Utilize the strengths of the team by getting out of the way more often.

Reflect & Write: Over to you. With the benefit of hindsight, reflect on five setbacks from your past. What were they? What was the root cause for each? What incorrect assumptions did you make? What have you learnt?

You see, with every setback there is a rich lesson to be learnt. As long as we pause to reflect and habitually look for the lessons in setbacks, we grow, and there is genuinely no failure to fear. You can simply celebrate knowing more about the world, other people, or yourself.

Course Correction

Consider a live project that isn't going to plan. Run it through the analysis that you've just used for past setbacks.

Reflect & Write: Complete the following sentences: *My reflection is... The root cause is ... My incorrect assumption is ... I've learnt that...* For this project, based on what you have learnt, create an updated version of your plan: *I will now...*

Just as companies constantly monitor and adjust their sales activity, so you will need to constantly review and correct your course of action. It's simply part of the process.

Fast Feedback Loops

When launching a new product, traditional companies follow a traditional process: market research to establish a customer need; test prototypes with focus groups; design the finished product; invest in the manufacturing process; build launch stock; advertise; sell; measure sales and establish feedback; course correct. The challenge for most companies is that the time from design to feedback is long, and the costs to course-correct are prohibitive. Therefore, it's a big bet that they are making based on the initial feedback from a relatively small focus group.

During the height of the space race in the 1960s, legend has it, NASA scientists realized that pens could not function in space. They needed to figure out another way for the astronauts to write things down. So they spent

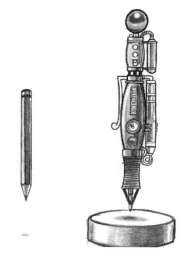

years and millions of taxpayer dollars to develop a pen that could put ink to paper without gravity. But their crafty Soviet counterparts, so the story goes, simply handed their cosmonauts pencils.[39]

There is another way.

In his best-selling book, *The Lean Start-up*,[40] Eric Ries advocates an innovative approach. Rather than developing a finished product, how do you get a prototype into the market quickly? He called this an MVP (minimum viable product), and the aim is to learn something about the most critical assumptions that are baked into the forecast. Using this technique, companies can iterate their product many times within a short time before investing significant capital on manufacturing at scale and advertising.

How is this relevant to you?

Looking back to your five EXACT goals, you have baked some big assumptions into them. It is better to test these early in your plan rather than to get halfway down the road only to find a roadblock (and then wishing you'd done something slightly different at the start).

Let me give you an example. I run live events based around the topics in this book, and it's partly the peer-to-peer interaction that makes them so powerful. I also write a monthly newsletter that contains links to interesting videos, blogs, cartoons and articles. I like to be innovative, working with smartphone technology to keep things fresh and interesting, and am used to recording short video clips.

When I first decided to write a book, it wasn't simply a book that was in the plan. It was a full multimedia experience that blended together with a physical journal, an app, professionally shot videos and a chat forum. It had everything! The scale was excitingly ambitious, and I began to develop a funding strategy. Then I remembered the principles from *The Lean Start-up*.

Using a mock-up, I was able to quickly get feedback from a target user group. The results were clear. It's too complicated. Yes, give me a physical book, make it enticing by limiting the amount of text I need to wade through, and use illustrations to land the key points more powerfully. But don't do the app, and don't put QR codes into the book which trigger videos to load on your phone.

My initial reaction was disappointment, 'Why don't people like my awesome idea?' But thank goodness I listened. I could have wasted a couple of years and tens of thousands of pounds on something that people don't like.

Reflect & Write: Considering your five EXACT goals, what are the big assumptions that you are making and how can you test them soon?

Gratitude for Setbacks

In the previous chapter, you plotted a graph that represented the ups and downs of a project that made you proud. Would you have been as proud of yourself if you hadn't had to endure some hardships? Pushing through difficulties is really fulfilling. If we never experienced setbacks, could we be proud of anything? Every experience, no matter how bad it seems, contains a gift to be unwrapped.

STRIVING VS EXPERIENCING

Imagine that each letter on this page represents a week of your life, which means that by the time you get to the end of this sentence, you are about three years old. As you keep reading, each decade is marked [in square brackets], and remember that the global average life expectancy is 70 years.

Pause at the paragraph that contains your current age. That's how much of your life has passed already. Life is flying by.

When I first read a blog called 'Your Life in Weeks'[41] by one of my favourite bloggers, Tim Urban, it caused me to pause and reflect on the passing of time. [Age 10] He describes each week as precious, like a shining diamond, and there are only two good ways to spend your diamond:

1. Enjoy the diamond.
2. Build something to make your future diamonds more enjoyable.

Throughout this chapter, we've focussed on number 2 – building future shiny diamond weeks. However, living a life purely on building for the future misses the point of life. Life can only be experienced in the present moment (remember mindfulness from page 100). [Age 20]

In many ways, my wife and I are opposites. I like to plan our holidays, doing the research and booking things – I'm a natural planner. The problem is that when I'm on holiday, my mind can wander into planning what is coming next rather than really experiencing the great moment that exists right now. My wife lives in the moment, totally consumed by the experience of the now. [Age 30]

During our South Africa road trip (that I was dreaming about back on page 93) we found ourselves sitting on the cliffs of the best land-based whale-watching site in the world (Hermanus). While my body was sitting, my mind wasn't resting. It was concerned with the clock and what time we'd need to leave to get to a restaurant for dinner. In front of us, a whale leapt out of the sea, flipped, and splash landed. 'Did you just see that?' my wife asked.

'See what?' I replied.

So while we're working on the practices to Own Life, please also listen to my wife's advice to me: *'Don't miss life by constantly building for the future, it's OK to simply enjoy the diamonds too.'* [Age 40]

Concluding Thoughts

Dreams will remain dreams unless they are turned into powerfully motivating goals. Goals will remain unachieved unless they are planned. Plans will remain undelivered unless they are re-planned. Failures will remain failures unless they are learnt from. There's a formula involved in making dreams a reality, and you have the formula written down in this chapter. Whatever you want to achieve, if you run it through the formula, you will be successful. [Age 50]

CHAPTER 6
MANAGING TIME

If you don't manage your relationship with time, then others will: boss, colleagues, family, neighbours, children, and social media algorithms. A good time manager is conscious of the value of their time, deliberately decides what to do with it and spends it efficiently by doing important things. By the end of this chapter, you'll have a set of techniques that put you in control of whatever time remains in your life. Stephen Covey summarizes our goal nicely: *'The challenge is not to manage time, but to manage ourselves.'*

TIME: THE MOST PRECIOUS RESOURCE

Consider your life to be the length of a candle, each moment that passes, the flame burns away a little wax. We don't notice each minute that passes, but puff – there it goes. Only after considerable time has passed do we notice that the candle of life has shrunk. Did the past moments simply melt away, or did they bring light and warmth to your memories? Time is the only commodity that can't be replenished. When it's gone, it's gone. When your candle burns downs, this lifetime for you, is over. And while we can imagine that our candle may last 70 years or more, the reality is that the flame sometimes gets snuffed out early.

Life can be viewed as a beautiful candle, but it is really about the dancing flame that burns moment to moment. Only when we realize that each minute of our time is a little part of our life and that there is no guarantee that there will be another one, will we truly value it as we should.

In this chapter, you'll learn some powerful time management tools, but they'll only be effective if you are ready to truly value your time and fight for it. If you have the right attitude, then read on.

HOW WISELY DO YOU USE TIME NOW
Black Belt or Black Hole?

We all know someone who seems to get more done than there are hours in the day. My friend Damian runs a couple of successful businesses, sits on the board of three schools, runs extreme ultra-marathons, has four kids, and always has time for a coffee. Oh, and he's training for his karate black belt. You could say that he's a black belt in time management.

You'll also know someone at the other end of the spectrum. Rather than having a black belt, time seems to slip down a black hole. I met a guy last weekend who retired at 50 years old with plenty of money in the bank, no children or elderly relatives; he was an engaging storyteller with a bubbly personality and in good physical health. I asked what he'd been up to in the three years since he retired. And then I kept on probing because I couldn't find an answer. In the end, it got a little awkward as I tried not to let my judgement show by getting transparently overenthusiastic about how lovely his frequently mown lawn must be. The candle had burned down a long way, and there wasn't a single remarkable memory. The wax had disappeared into a black hole. Who do you know whose time seems to slip through their fingers?

Reflect & Write: Consider which of your friends is a time black belt, and which is a time black hole?

Reflect & Write: Where do you sit? Put an 'x' on the line somewhere, and then write down why (capturing in your own words how you are sometimes wise and sometimes foolish with your time).

BLACK HOLE   BLACK BELT

Black Belt Training Plan

Let's break things down a little as multiple elements come together to make a black belt. Which of the following statements are true for you?

I always have a list of things I need to do written down in one place.	True / False
I set aside sufficient time to do the most important things.	True / False
I am good at saying 'no' to people who want my time.	True / False
I don't procrastinate.	True / False
Every day, I am clear about my priorities.	True / False
I am organized and effective at planning future activities.	True / False
When I've made a plan, I stick with it and see things through to the end.	True / False
I easily strike off low-value activities. I don't waste time.	True / False
I control my time.	True / False

If the statements are mainly true for you, then you're most of the way there: you have some good habits, and perhaps simply need a couple more to truly be a black belt. If they are mainly false, then I have two pieces of great news for you. The first is that your future can be immeasurably more rewarding and fulfilling than your past. And the second is that everything you need is contained in the next few sections.

TIME PLANNING
The Humble 'To-do' List

My wife pokes fun at my list-making – which is fine. My list is written down in one place. It contains ALL the things I need to do whether they are work or life-related. It is always up to date, and I refer to it to plan my activities. I trust the system I have in place, and I never forget to do anything. My wife too has a list. It resides

in her head and occasionally comes out in random sticky notes, or scribbles on the kitchen whiteboard. Her memory is much better than mine, but it's not as infallible as my list. She does occasionally forget to do things, and because of this, she worries about forgetting to do things, which leads to stress.

The humble to-do list is the most basic step towards good time management. Once it is in place, you can add layers of sophistication to get towards your black belt. If you don't currently have a list, here are my top tips for making the to-do list work for you. If you already have a to-do list, check off which strategies you already employ:

It's in one place: There is just one list, it may be subdivided with headings for different categories, but it is all in the same format, in the same place. (I have experimented with a range of different methods of categorization and have found that simplicity works best for me. I have one list that is my 'work' list, and one list that is my 'home jobs'.)

Nothing is missed: Everything goes on the list the moment it arises, nothing is left to memory. (I always have a notebook out on the table during meetings or conversations and use the @ symbol in the margin to highlight any actions I record which need transferring to the to-do list.)

Everything is a simple action: Send meter reading. Fit new cupboard catch. Call electrician. Check the annual cost of house alarm versus ADT & Yale. There's no ambiguity about what I have to do next, or when I get the simple pleasure of striking it off the list. Avoid putting projects on the list – 'learn French' isn't a simple action. 'Research apps for learning French' is.

I'm wholly responsible: There's nothing on the list that relies on someone else.

I've made the decision to do it: Before I write anything down, I take a very important step: I've made a judgement that I intend to do it. (We'll cover this in some detail in the next section as it's critically important to success.)

Two-minute rule: If it takes less than two minutes, just do it, don't add it to the list.

Future to-do's go on the calendar: Certain things need to happen on a specific date, so instead of putting them on the list and then having to remember when they need doing, put them into your calendar. 'Send Andy a birthday card', is better on a specific date in the calendar rather than sitting on the to-do list for 360 days!

In a moment it's over to you to create your list or update your existing one. What you use to capture the list is up to you. Pen and paper have worked for generations, and many people swear by it. I'm an Apple user, so use the Reminders app since it syncs across my devices, and I like the simplicity of it. You may want something with greater functionality so Google 'best to-do list apps' and take your pick of the free tools on offer.

Reflect & Write: There's not much more to say about it, let's not turn writing a list into rocket science. Choose where you will record your list, follow the simple tips above and get listing.

Saying 'No'

OK, so you have your list. With everything on it, right? You know you've got everything because any time your mind says 'I must remember to…' you can smile because it's on the list and you don't have to remember anything ;-)

I bet your list looks pretty long now, daunting perhaps. Don't worry about it. It may be the first time you've seen everything laid out in black and white. Now you have the full picture of what you have to do, you can move onto prioritising and scheduling things so that you feel in full control. Previously, this full list has probably been swimming around in your head with random tasks occasionally flashing up in lights in your full consciousness at random (and often unhelpful) times.

Before you move onto tackling this list, you have to ensure that the to-do list remains live and workable. It's a complete list at this moment. But pretty soon something will arise that you'd forgotten to add to the list. It would be unusual for the list not to change in any 24 hours. If you add more to the list than you strike off, then simple maths tells us that the list gets longer. If you are to stay in control of your list, then you simply can't accept more tasks than you can cross off. If your list is longer than can be accomplished, you're going to let yourself and other people down. You'll feel like you're never in control. Like a hamster in a wheel, spinning around and not getting anywhere. Guilty. Stressed.

If you can't control what goes on the list, then all the time management tools will prove useless. A single two-letter word is your key to a fulfilling life. That word is 'no'. 'No' to the requests of other people. 'No' to yourself when facing temptations. Perhaps you have an inner voice that says, 'I can't say no'; yet you also have evidence that you can and do say no without it hurting other people or causing you stress. When do you assertively say 'no'?

You know when you go to a restaurant, possibly an Italian, and the waiter approaches wielding an oversized pepper grinder asking, 'Black pepper?' and you say 'No, thank you'. That's the feeling that you're looking for when saying no to other people who attempt to overdose your plate with ingredients that you don't want.

Of course, 'no' has consequences, some of which can be softened. The consequence of autopilot 'yes' to everyone and everything is lifelong suffering. So why do we do it? Why do you?

Reflect & Write: Complete this sentence: *I sometimes find it hard to say 'no' to other people because...*

It takes practice to say 'no' in a way that is assertive enough to be understood by the other person, and yet respectful enough to leave no long-term damage to your important relationships. Take a look at what's on your to-do list. You've accepted these things, and there is an expectation that they will be delivered; therefore it's awkward, but perhaps not impossible, to backtrack and now say 'no'. Each relationship and each task is different so you will need to adapt the language and choose the moment, but it may be possible for you to experiment with something like:

> *'I accepted this task from you, and now I realize that I have taken on too much and won't be able to complete it to a standard that I'd be happy with. I apologize. Could we have a chat about reassigning it?'*

Would this be better than sticking your head in the sand and hoping the other person forgets? Or struggling to produce something of poor quality? Or not doing something else of greater importance? You may have no option but to follow through on some things on your list that, with hindsight, you wish you hadn't accepted. But you can use these as case studies to learn from.

Reflect & Write: Consider five things that you have said 'yes' to, when you wish you had said 'no'. A similar situation may arise again, so how will you tackle it next time? How will you say, respectfully and assertively, 'no'?

If you're empathetic, then you may already be putting yourself in the other person's shoes and feeling a little hurt by hearing yourself say 'no'. That's good. You have emotional intelligence. If you didn't, then your no's could be genuinely hurtful, and you'd forget to balance assertiveness with respect. But the reality is that receiving a 'no' however it is dressed up, is less pleasant than receiving a 'yes, I'd love to help you out, tell me what I can do for you'. This is why we can get trapped in a people pleasing busyness loop that ultimately helps no one. Let's not hide the fact; protecting your time by saying 'no' takes courage, and a degree of selfishness.

Reflect & Write: Complete this sentence: *I am/am not ready to find sufficient courage and selfishness to say 'no' more often because...*

Time management requires you to be responsible for your time, which means that you need to be able to respond to other people's demands on it. Summing up by using the words of Warren Buffet, 'really successful people say no to virtually everything'.

Saying 'No' to Yourself

There's a ton of stuff I'd like to do, and I could easily double my list of 'home jobs' within five minutes. I know I don't have the time to get them all done so when the idea arises in my mind I'm making a conscious choice to a) put it on the list and drop something else, b) accept that it will never happen and forget it, c) add it to the list titled 'for some other time'. Most things on the 'c' list never come off it as they never become high enough priority to trump something else, but I feel happier I've recorded it as an option.

Reflect & Write: When looking at your to-do list now, are there any things that you feel would be better suited to a separate list titled 'for some other time'? Or any that you really should simply say 'no' to, and strike off immediately?

Make Space for the Big Rocks

There was a philosophy professor who was giving a lecture[42]. In front of him, he had a big glass jar. He started off by filling up the jar with big rocks, and when they reached the rim of the jar, he held it up to the students and asked them if the jar was full. They all agreed, there was no more room to put the rocks in, it was full.

He then picked up a tub of small pebbles and poured them into the jar so they filled the space around the big rocks. 'Is the jar full now?' he asked. The group of students all looked at each other and agreed that the jar was now completely full.

The professor then picked up another container, this time, it had sand in it. He poured the sand in between the pebbles and the rocks and once again, he held up the jar to his class and asked if it was full. Once again, the students agreed that the jar was full.

'Are you sure it's full?' he asked. He finally picked up a bottle of water and tipped the water into the jar until it filled up all the remaining space. The students laughed.

The professor went on to explain that the jar represents everything in one's life. The rocks are equivalent to the most important things you have going on, such as spending time with your family and maintaining proper health. This means that if the pebbles and the sand were lost, the jar would still be full, and your life would still have meaning.

The pebbles represent the things in your life that matter, but that you could live without. The pebbles certainly give your life meaning (such as your job, house, hobbies and friendships), but they are not critical for you to have a meaningful life. These things often come and go and are not permanent or essential to your overall wellbeing.

Finally, the sand represents the remaining filler things in your life. This could be small things such as watching television or running errands. These things don't mean much to your life as a whole and are likely only done to waste time or get small tasks accomplished.

If the professor began filling the jar with sand, and then added the pebbles, there wouldn't be space for all the life-critical big rocks. Yet this is often how we live our lives.

Reflect & Write: What are the big rocks that underpin the foundation of your life? You may have already written some of them down in this journal. Choose five to seven of them.

Reflect & Write: The pebbles are significant things that you have going on in your life now. What examples do you have? Go for 10–20 of them.

Everything else that consumes your time is sand. The question now is: are you giving the right amount of attention to each category? Your time might feel full, but is it full of sand? Are the pebbles and rocks getting the space they need?

Start with the rocks, and keeping things simple so just using your gut feeling, select one of the rocks and ask –

does it get the time that its importance deserves? Tick the yes's and estimate the time you spend on them. For the no's make a note of how much time you consider is necessary. Now do the same with the pebbles.

You may find that one or more subjects gets a very firm tick; it could be a rock. Is it absorbing too much attention at the detriment of others? Could you allow yourself to release some time from it without a negative impact?

You're likely to be looking at a mixed bag; some ticks, some crosses. You also have the total number of hours that you need in a month to pay sufficient attention to all of your rocks and pebbles. Can they fit into the number of waking hours that you have at your disposal? Do they fit into your jar?

If the answer is no, then return to your list of rocks and pebbles and throw out the least important ones until the remainder fit. Don't be tempted to squeeze the time for each one to make it fit – by definition, you will simply be assigning insufficient time to everything. If it fits, but it's tight, that's fine. The professor's jar looked full, but in reality, there was always space for more little things.

Now it's simply a matter of allocating time to your rocks and pebbles and sticking to it. For me, this includes:

- Blocking two full days per week to write this book for the next six months.
- On Sundays, discussing with my wife when I will fit my six exercise sessions around our family commitments.
- Not accepting any phone calls before 9am to allow me to walk my son to school each day.

Stephen Covey simplifies it nicely: *'The key is not to prioritize what's on your schedule but to schedule your priorities.'*

Reflect & Write: So back to you and your list of pebbles and rocks. When precisely, will you do each of them? How will you schedule them? Grab your calendar and spend the next 30 minutes making your schedule for the next month or more.

Sifting the Sand

Looking back at the last month, write down everything you've spent time doing that isn't directly connected with one of your rocks or pebbles. There will inevitably be space to squeeze in some sand, so sift your list to select which sand you enjoy and want to keep. Circle each grain that you want to retain in your life, and then give it an amount of time that you want to spend doing it. For example, I want to keep reading the BBC News app for 30 minutes a day; and I want to fritter away 15 minutes flicking through Facebook.

There's no need to get completely into the detail of the sand – just notice your intention to limit the amount of time you spend on each activity, and then set a reminder in your calendar every month to spend 10 minutes returning to this page to check your reality versus your intention, and update your intentions for the following month.

Reflect & Write: Complete this sentence: *The sand of my life includes...*

Prioritization

Dig out the to-do list you made earlier. Is the action related to a rock (R), pebble (P), or sand (S)? Prefix the action with an R, P, or S. Your list now has a rank of relative importance and you can use it to plot your tasks on the Y-axis of the Eisenhower Matrix.

Eisenhower recognized that *'what is important is seldom urgent and what is urgent is seldom important'*. Stephen Covey popularized the Eisenhower matrix, and it has become a widely used tool to help prioritize tasks using a visual scale of urgency and importance.[43]

Box 1 activities are your immediate priority – the most important things in life, which you are doing under intense time pressure. It's a recipe for stress rather than quality work. Your goal is to minimize the amount of time that you spend here. Here's how:

- Stop procrastinating on projects with deadlines.
- Push back on last-minute demands of others. Is it important to you? Is it really as urgent as it is made out to be? Would the requester prefer higher quality in the future, or a fast turnaround now?
- Schedule and protect the time for your rocks and pebbles (box 2).

Crises will emerge from time to time, and that's just life. Your goal is to be in the non-crisis mode most of the time so that when a genuine one arises you are in good health to tackle it with all of your energy.

Reflect & Write: Looking down all the Rs and Ps on your to-do list, which are also urgent? How did they become urgent, and what can you resolve to do in the future to reduce the time you spend in stressful box 1?

Box 2 is where you want to spend most of your time. Doing the most important things to a high quality. It's also the most commonly neglected quadrant: the rewards aren't as immediate; there is usually less pressure coming from other people; they require more energy than box 4 actions, and the consequences for not doing them may lie over the horizon.

Reading and completing this book is a good example of a box 2 activity. Is anyone else pushing you to do it? No. Would it make a massive difference if you didn't do it for another year? No. Would it be easy to give up the time you are spending on it to do something else from box 3 or 4? Yes. You can see how easy it is for box 2 activities to get squashed. It is the reason why we have already scheduled your rocks and pebbles.

Reflect & Write: Assume that you can fight to protect your box 2 time, and genuinely give appropriate time to your rocks and pebbles. Now complete this sentence: *When I give sufficient time to the most important things in my life, I will...*

Box 3 is where you feel busy, but don't seem to get anything significant done. It's the things on your to-do list that got there because of an autopilot 'yes'. By effectively and respectfully applying the word 'no' more frequently, you will be able to reduce the time you are spending in this box. Also, reduce interruptions by turning off your email notifications and only accessing them twice per day; put your phone in flight mode when focussing on a task; temporarily move out of an open-plan space into a side office, work from home, or put in earphones. The final tip is to stop and consider if you're doing something out of habit or because 'it's the way it's always been done'.

While it may feel good to be needed, and 'to always be there for people when they need me', it comes at a high-efficiency cost. It is possible to protect your box 2 focus AND be available to others as long as you take responsibility for when you can give them 100 per cent of your attention, rather than allowing others to dictate when they can steal your focus and receive your partial attention.

Reflect & Write: Complete this sentence: *My strategies to reduce the time I spend in box 3 are...*

Box 4 is full of sand. You go here for light relief after spending too much time on the left-hand urgent, stressful side of the matrix. We can be OK with some time-wasting, can't we? You've sifted your sand to allow the best bits through and restricted the amount of time spent in box 4 by setting time limits that you will track monthly. By the way, you do need to recharge your batteries; if some element of 'energy management' isn't one of your rocks or pebbles already then I'm sure it will be by the time you have completed Chapter 7. 'Personal Care' is a box 2 activity.

You now have a to-do list that contains EVERYTHING, and no longer need to rely on memory. You have a diary that is planned to give you sufficient time for the most important elements of your life. You have some strategies to reduce the amount of time you're operating with a feeling of urgency, and an intention to be very conscious about when you say 'yes' and sometimes finding ways to say 'no'. You have a plan. Black-belt celebration time! Or is it?

No, not just yet.

If you've never planned your time this way, then sure, pause and give yourself a mini reward as it's not an intuitive or fun process for many people. Remember back to the last chapter. The plan that you have right now is simply your best estimate, based on the knowledge that you have available to you. As you begin to live it, you'll get more data, and be able to refine the plan. Honing it takes time, so keep iterating it. Failure is simply feedback, so when you learn through experience, just make the plan better. Once you've paused for the pat on the back, it's time to take the next step towards back-belt mastery. You have to execute the plan, and that starts with overcoming this little thing called 'procrastination'.

PROCRASTINATION

Procrastinating means 'postponing important tasks and replacing them with less important ones that are more fun and easier to do'. Given this definition, it's a wonder that we don't procrastinate all of the time on everything!

Whatever you are doing, at any moment I could tempt you to stop by offering you something that was more fun and easier.

We are all, by nature, procrastinators. It's just that some people have learnt techniques to overcome the temptation of instant gratification and have developed the ability to persevere with long-term challenging (but important) activities.

Procrastinators often find themselves in a place of self-loathing, it's one trait that they wish that they could magic away. But why is this? To non-procrastinators, they seem to have a wonderful 'carefree' attitude to life but dig a little deeper, and we begin to understand how debilitating it can be.

It comes down to a constant inner voice that says, 'You should be...'

You should be doing that assignment, you should be looking for a better job, you should be down the gym, you should be reading more books, you should call your mum, you should be making more of your life. Even when the procrastinator is playing, because the playtime hasn't been earnt, it's not deeply fun.

But the procrastinator cannot stop having this 'fake fun' until it's too late. A deadline looms large, panic sets in, and they work frantically to get the job done. But it is just done, not done well, and so procrastinators move into a self-critical phase of loathing.

And it gets worse! For when there isn't a deadline set by the outside world, the procrastinators can't set their own. Therefore no panic, no frantic working, and no results at all.

Far from Owning Life, the life of a procrastinator is passing by without achieving anything on their 'I really want' list, producing sub-standard work in a panic, and having lots of 'fake-fun'.

The Eisenhower Connection

You may already have made the link. The procrastinator loves box 4, playing in the sand that doesn't really matter, isn't very hard, and feels like fun. The rational human wants to execute the plan you just made and live most of its time in box 2 – calmly doing the things that really matter, spending appropriate time on the rocks and the pebbles. For some of these activities, there is an external deadline, so things inevitably shift into box 1, and get started.

Yes You Are a Procrastinator

When you considered what was in your box 1, and contemplated the cause of it being there, for some of you the main cause will be procrastination. When given a project you don't work through it methodically, you can't seem to get started until it's almost too late; when the panic sets in.

Circle which one applies to you: I find myself panicking: never / occasionally / sometimes / frequently / every day.

Perhaps you've circled 'never', perhaps you do diligently begin work when it is issued and conscientiously work through it steadily. Nice job, you are managing your time effectively on time-critical activities and avoiding undue stress.

What about those important things that don't have an externally imposed deadline? There will be no moment of panic. No sudden burst of energy to get started. They can be put off forever, and I bet you've already put a handful of them off.

Like what? Like: quitting the job, changing careers, ditching sour people, stop smoking, start exercising, making the doctor's appointment, saying 'I love you', going on a date, enrolling on a course, decluttering the house, giving feedback, getting a dog, writing a book, starting a business, blogging, volunteering, running a marathon, calling a relative, standing up to the boss, going travelling, putting up a LinkedIn profile.

Reflect & Write: Your turn. What are you avoiding doing?

The ONLY Painkiller

If you find yourself in the not-actually-fun fun place, you'll know that it's a painful place to be. You also know, from experience, that the pain begins to subside once you finally get on with the thing that you've been procrastinating about. In fact, it's the only pain relief that is available. As soon as you cross the Action Line, the pain begins to subside.

In fact, being in the middle of procrastination is often *more painful* than being in the middle of doing the work. Point A on the chart below is often more painful than Point B. The guilt, shame, and anxiety that you feel while procrastinating is usually worse than the effort and energy you have to put in while you're working. The problem isn't *doing* the work, it's *starting* the work.[44]

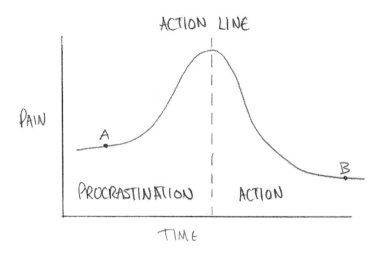

A Kick Up the Arse

So, all you need is a kick up the arse, like your mum used to give you when you stayed in bed till noon as a teenager, or when my wife reminds me to floss. But if your mum's not around, or if your instant gratification monkey isn't listening, you need a more grown-up set of strategies. Here's a bunch:

1. Micro-steps that establish momentum

Your journey may be long and difficult, but the very first tiny step is likely to be pretty straightforward. So take it without worrying about all the ones that come afterwards. After the first step is taken, the second one emerges and again, looks manageable. You get over the action line, you have momentum, and as the pain relief kicks in you find greater and greater energy. Just get unstuck by starting in a very small way.

2. Find joy in the short-term

Instant gratification can be your ally if you give it what it wants – short-term pleasure. Identifying little rewards that it can chase as it hits milestones on the journey towards the long-term goal. A progress chart works nicely, with little smiley faces next to the tasks completed. Got a report to write? Break it down: section headings drafted ☺, one hour of research on the first section ☺, first section roughly drafted ☺. Three smileys equal a Netflix episode this evening. Sounds a bit childish, right? Remember, it's your childish self that you're dealing with, not your rational adult self!

3. A token of success

You're sure that this task is one of the important ones in life, right? That's why you're stressing about it. There's a diamond that will be revealed after all this pressure. So, let's see how the diamond sparkles, and how much pleasure will come from it. When setting your goals earlier in the book, you imagined the future with wonderful colour and richness, you pre-lived the future rewards and experienced the emotional high of the finish line. You can give the short-term-focussed version of you an emotional high every day by keeping the diamond in sight. Find a token that represents the elation of completing your important task and ensure that you stumble across it every day. My friend splashed some cash and bought a personalized number plate that reminded him of his goal multiple times a day. Others I've worked with have used a photo on the desk, a crystal in the pocket, a card in the wallet, a bracelet, a special coffee cup. What token can you infuse with the pre-lived emotions of success?

4. Induce a minor panic

It's almost impossible to resist the influence of the panicked mind, so how can you lay bait for it to come out of hiding and give you the kick that you need? Last time I attempted to learn the guitar I shot a video of the final 2 minutes of my first practice session. Loaded it to YouTube and sent the link to all my friends with the message 'Watch me learn to play the guitar, new post coming every Friday until I've got 'Wonderwall' nailed'. The following Thursday (and every other Thursday) the panic monster surfaced, and I practised until my fingers were raw. The Friday video went out on time, and I got better at playing the guitar (until I realized that I had bigger rocks that needed attending to). What bait could you use to induce a minor panic?

5. Apply the growth mindset

Remember back to Chapter 2: reward effort rather than outcomes. Release yourself from chasing excellence, or a fear of imperfection. When doing yoga, my poses bear little resemblance to the YouTube instructor I'm attempting to mirror. When meditating, my monkey brain dances about wildly, and I rarely empty my mind for more than half a minute.

In comparison to others, my results are dishearteningly poor, but simply by showing up and trying my best, I feel better. Shifting the goal to 'effort' puts it within my capabilities. I can practice yoga for half an hour. How can you change your goal from outcome to effort?

6. Put the first things first

If you ranked your to-do list in order of importance, what comes in the first place? Put this first on your schedule for the day. In fact, start each day knowing the three things that will make the biggest difference and do them before allowing any box 3 or 4 activities to encroach on your time. If you get them done by lunchtime, take the afternoon off – you deserve it. If you don't the 'fun' insignificant stuff will fill your time, and you'll keep hanging out in the not-fun fun place.

7. Feel the fear and do it anyway[45]

You have a decision to take: Path A or Path B. Or you decide to procrastinate and stand still. You're worried that path A would lead to a series of imagined negative consequences, and path B would lead to a different set of negative outcomes, and you've been conditioned to fear making the 'wrong decision'. If you and your twin could lead parallel lives, one taking path A and the other, path B, you would be able to meet up in the future and assess which proved to be the 'right' path. And that would be possible if this was the only crossroad that you faced in life. But of course, path A branches into paths C, D, E, and F, and then each of those branch again. And it would be possible only if you had a twin. And it would only be useful if you could rewind time to back to the decision moment and correct a 'wrong' decision.

All of this, of course, is fantasy, and we live in a world of reality. When you stand at the decision point, it is impossible to accurately predict where the path leads with any certainty, and as you walk the path, new side routes will emerge that you can't see at the moment.

Yes, do the research to find out which path is likely to help you to achieve your short-term goals. And then go for it. You will feel the fear of making the 'wrong decision', but truly, the only wrong decision is to make no decision. So, 5,4,3,2,1, Start!

8. Push away distractions

Remember the willpower section? Those with seemingly strong self-control have a magic trick – they remove temptations. If you're addicted to checking your phone for social media titbits: lock it away; download an app that prevents its use before midday and give your partner the unlock code; do anything but leave the phone within arm's reach! Clear your desk of everything. Put your phone in flight mode. Turn your back to everyone else in the office or put in headphones. You know what tempts you away, so don't rely on your finite reserves of willpower, push it far far away.

9. Done means done

Don't stop until it's finished. Once you've pushed over the action line, keep going to the end. Don't let yourself off the hook, don't do a half job, stay with it until the end. Otherwise, you'll have to climb the inertia hill all over again. When you have momentum, don't squander it.

Reflect & Write: Choosing three topics that are important, and that you are procrastinating about (box 2 stuff), which of the grown-up procrastination fighting strategies feel right, and how will you specifically apply them?

Stopping the 'STOP' Before It Gets Started

A memory that is etched into my brain and generates an instant smile of pride is of a sunny Saturday in 2014. The sun was filtering through a canopy of trees which lined the side of the smooth path through our local park. My daughter took a deep breath, I steadied her, and she pushed off. Her bike gathering momentum as I walked, then jogged alongside her until she was racing away with me left in her wake, a huge smile on my face as she cycled on her own for the very first time. After 100 metres, she stopped and turned around with a smile as wide as my own. And then she couldn't get started again on her own. She got frustrated. And she cried.

When cycling, the hardest part is coordinating the push forwards from the ground, and the simultaneous downward pressure on the pedal while correcting the initial wobble by leaning the body and locating the second foot on the pedal for the next downward stroke. The second rotation of the feet is easier, and then the third. By the fourth and fifth, the momentum keeps you upright, the effort on the pedals is less, and the head can rise to enjoy the ride as a smile cracks across your face.

In the previous sections we focused on how to get started once procrastination has set in. It's possible of course, but energy-sapping – what if you could maintain a steady momentum? What if it always felt like you were taking the fifth pedal stroke instead of the first? The key is to make the following three steps part of your routine, every day of every week.

1. **Know your priorities:** Annually, monthly and weekly, check that your rocks, pebbles and sand haven't shifted.

2. **First things first:** The most important task (regardless of how challenging it may be), goes first on your list of actions for the day, and when I say first, I mean FIRST.

3. **Get it done:** Until the most important thing is done, it isn't done! It therefore remains your only focus, everything else is procrastination!

FINDING TIME
Dead Time

Let's oversimplify things. Imagine that time can be categorized into:

a) Things that take me closer to living a fulfilling life.
b) Things that recharge my batteries.
c) Other stuff.

Then estimate how much time you spend in each category. Which chart best represents your current life (by the way, sleeping is in the battery recharging category)?

So far in this book, you've been determining what's in the first category, and in this chapter, ensuring that they are planned so they happen. In the next chapter, you will be working on category b – defining the things that will bring you the energy you need to do the stuff that leads to a fulfilling life. Because you want to maximize your time for the first two categories, you need to minimize the time spent doing 'other stuff'. Since it isn't really contributing to life, you could call this 'dead time'.

Can you eliminate it entirely? Possibly not, but you can really really try! There are some essentials, such as grocery

THINGS THAT TAKE ME
CLOSER TO LIVING A
FULFILLING LIFE

THINGS THAT RECHARGE
MY BATTERIES

OTHER STUFF

shopping, housework, commuting, personal hygiene, household paperwork, or dropping children to school. And some non-essentials – the sand of life.

Reflect & Write: You've already done some work to filter the sand, look back to page 165, how much dead time will you be recovering by leaving the sand behind?

Go back to those essentials and see if you can find a way to move them from the dead zone to the life zone. You can't eliminate them, so can you reframe them?

Reflect & Write: Considering all the time you spend in the dead zone, what activity takes up the most time? Can you identify your top non-productive time consumers? Create a table and list them in column 1, and then in column 2, estimate what percentage of the total dead time it consumes (the total should add up to 100 per cent, and for now, leave a third column blank).

Now we know where all the dead time is, we can begin to look at how it may be possible to use it more productively, by doing the essential task while also achieving progress towards our fulfilling life or recharging our batteries.

In a moment it will be time to get creative, to decide what could work for you, and to get you warmed up, here are some examples from my life:

Travelling: Today is the 20th of January, and so far this year I have travelled from my home in Essex to Edinburgh in Scotland, and then Singapore. Right now as I type these words, I am sitting on a balcony overlooking the sea, a stiffening breeze blowing the trees and keeping the humidity at bay, a breeding pair of white-bellied sea eagles circling overhead, and the noise a combination of construction workers and flights taking off just over my right shoulder. By the time I walk in my door at home tomorrow morning, I will have spent about 35 hours travelling so far this year, representing seven per cent of the total time that has passed since the New Year began. In comparison, since the start of the year, I have spent fewer than five hours immersed in play with my five-year-old son. How can I bring life to the dead time of travelling? If you're a commuter, you have the same opportunity.

Here's how I will get home. On the 15-minute ride from my hotel to the airport, I intend to engage the driver in conversation and find out something about life in Singapore. I arrive at the airport three hours before the flight leaves so there is no queue at check-in, and I accept 15 minutes of dead time at the check-in counter as I drop my bags off. I have a podcast cued up on my phone that will take me through the standard queue at security. Once through I find a chair in the waiting area, logon to the WiFi, plug in my earphones, select an album from Napster, set the alarm on my phone, and then immerse myself in writing this book for 90 minutes. I'll then eat a substantial dinner and go back to the podcast while waiting at the departure gate to board the plane.

I've imagined the entire journey to my front door, and I have made sure that I have the resources I need. The vast majority of my 15-hour return journey isn't dead time, it is either working towards a fulfilling life (writing the book) or recharging my batteries (eating and podcast listening). So, while I have spent 35 hours travelling, only five hours is dead time, the rest sits in one of the other two categories. What about things other than travelling?

- Walking my son to school is dad-son bonding time.
- Brushing my teeth in the morning is the moment I confirm my priorities for the day.
- Cooking is 'me' time with my choice of music when my mind can wander wherever it likes.

Reflect & Write: Over to you. Go back to the table you created and complete column three. Instead of considering the time 'dead time', how can you reframe it so that it becomes 'alive time'? Get creative. How do you feel now?

Growing Influence by Shrinking Concern

Earth orbits the sun and spins on its axis 365 days per year, 24 hours per day, ad infinitum. You can't control time. You can exert some control over yourself, you can influence many things, and for everything else, you exert no influence at all.

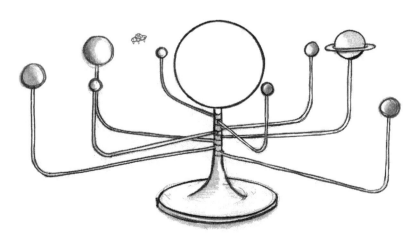

When you are spending time in your sphere of influence, you are proactively living your life. When you are expending time and energy outside of it, you are consuming valuable resources without any positive benefit. Stephen Covey[46] labelled the 'non-influencing zone' as the 'sphere of concern'. Here, we are reactive, negative, and slipping into a 'victim mentality'. The goal is to reduce the amount of time and energy spent in this zone so that you can expend more energy on the things that you *can* influence, thereby taking more control of your life. There are two ways of reducing the size of your sphere of concern: let it go; or get resourceful.

What kinds of things fit in the sphere of concern?

- Worries about friends or family members
- Gossip
- World affairs such as politics, the economy or global warming
- The plot of soap operas and reality TV shows
- Inner-voice reconstructions of past arguments

In short, it's everything that consumes our thoughts but doesn't lead to an intention to take action that would make a difference.

Reflect & Write: What is on the list for you? What things consume thought, yet you take no action about?

You can now choose to keep those things because they are serving you positively in some way, or eliminate them by applying one of two strategies:

'Let It Go'

Cue the famous song from Disney's film *Frozen*. Elsa, on the mountain top releasing herself from the shackles of pretending to be the little girl everyone believes her to be, releasing the power that she holds inside. In an explosive burst of energy, away from the need to conform, she becomes the woman that she is supposed to be, while singing, 'Let it Go' at full volume.

On your 'sphere of concern' list above, what can you let go of?

A technique that I've found useful when trying to release my brain from recycling old negative stories over and over again is simply to try to write it down. I sit with a pen thinking it will take page after page of notetaking, and yet most commonly after just a couple of paragraphs, I realize that I've captured everything that matters on the subject. My most common reaction when I see it in black and white is 'Is that it?'

Reflect & Write: Give it a go now, take one of the things that you are deciding to let go of, let the pen flow and write down everything that's been spinning around in your head. How does it feel now? Has is reduced its hold on you? Or perhaps you've come to the conclusion that there is some action you would now like to take?

Get Resourceful

The second strategy for getting out of your sphere of concern is to bring whatever it is into your sphere of influence by deciding to take action. You can make a difference if you choose to. Which of your previous list would you like to take action on?

- Global politics? Join a political party or a protest.
- Environmental impact? Give to charity, organize a litter-picking event, educate your children, avoid single-use plastic.
- Broken relationship? Extend an olive branch, practice forgiveness (more on this in Chapter 8).

Reflect & Write: OK. Back to your list, what do you now choose to take action on, and what action do you intend to take?

By reducing the time you spend being concerned and increasing the time you spend influencing, you are taking greater control of your life – it's motivating and inspiring, both for you and for those people who see you do it.

Concluding Thoughts

Switch on a computer, give it a task, and you can expect it to bring all of its available processing power from the first minute to the last. It's not the same for humans – we get tired.

In Formula One racing, every team schedules pit stops in every race, to replace the worn tyres with fresh ones. It may lose them 30 seconds, yet they are willing to give up the time, and sometimes even their lead in the race, because they know that as the tyres deteriorate, they get slower and slower every lap. In order to get to the finish line, they build in recovery time.

Throughout the day, your energy gets depleted, and without building in recovery time, you won't get to the end, or if you do, you'll be limping along at a snail's pace. Time management is important; energy management is essential! It's the subject of our next chapter.

Choosing what to do with your energy so that you make the most of every ounce of it is a matter of time management. You can't do everything that you'd like to, and other people will place demands on you that you can't control. While it's important to be deliberate about where you spend your time, don't get frustrated when reality doesn't perfectly fit the plan – that's life!

Amongst the great teachings of 2,000 years ago, Roman philosopher Seneca the Younger shared his wisdom: *'No person hands out their money to a passer-by, but to how many do each of us hand out our lives!'* To Own Life requires you to own your time.

CHAPTER 7
ENERGY AND RESILIENCE

Now that you are deliberate about how to use your time, it's time to manage the energy you bring to it. If you're low on energy, it doesn't matter how much time you have, your progress will be slow and unrewarding, and your motivation will wane.

In their brilliant book, *The Power of Full Engagement* Jim Loehr and Tony Schwartz suggest that '*performance, health and happiness are grounded in the skilful management of energy.*'[47] To Own Life and take control of the future requires us to take responsibility for the energy we bring to each moment of every day.

How energized do you feel right now? What if you track your level of energy over a day, a week or a month? When do you feel most energized, and what would you be able to accomplish if you could sustain it day-by-day over a lifetime? In this chapter, you will find out that it is possible, and how.

THE POWER OF ENERGY
Sharpen the Saw[48]

I sometimes wonder what alternative career I could have had, and I have this romantic idea that I would have enjoyed being a carpenter. One that makes fine furniture with gorgeous inlays that celebrate the natural beauty of the wood. To my fantasy I add that my converted barn workshop sits in the countryside made famous by the paintings of John Constable, and I would receive commissions from nobility across Europe. Oh, and it's the 16th century, and King Henry VIII is on the English throne.

Just occasionally, I try to live a little of this fantasy in my real life – and begin a carpentry project. My last such project was to build an 'L' shaped bench seat out of West African iroko wood for the patio of our garden. I treated myself to a brand-new set of chisels, watched a bunch of YouTube videos on how to use them, and took out my trusty handsaw that once belonged to my dad. The wood was delivered, and with a big smile and loads of enthusiasm, I began to saw it into the right lengths.

About an hour later with less than one per cent of the work done, my arm ached, and I was grateful to my wife for bringing me a cup of tea, and the comment 'Is that all you've done? It's going to take you forever!'

To which I replied, 'I know, this saw is a bit blunt, but I just want to crack on and get started rather than waste time going to get a new one.'

This is a personal story which mirrors the story told by Stephen Covey to illustrate the final habit in his book *The 7 Habits of Highly Effective People* which he calls 'sharpen the saw', in which he reminds us: *'We must never become too busy sawing to take time to sharpen the saw.'*

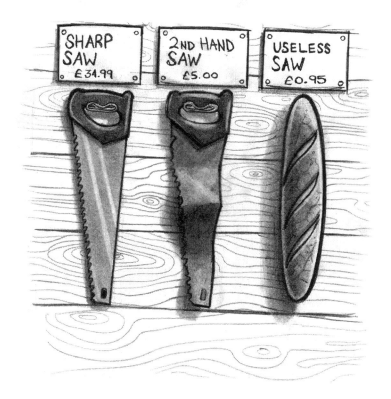

How Sharp Is Your Saw?

Last night, the kids were safely tucked up in bed, my wife was craving a horror movie fix (which isn't my cup of tea), and I sat down to read a few chapters of a book (a new Jack Reacher thriller by Lee Child), before going to bed at a sensible time. Some time later my wife came into the room, 'Have you been reading all this time?' Wow, Yes. Two hours had simply disappeared. I was so immersed in the story I'd completely lost any sense of time. I looked at the clock in disbelief – it was way past my regular bedtime and I wasn't yet ready to put the book down.

There are certain things that we do in life when time

seems to disappear. Your energy feels higher at the end than it did at the start, and it's a challenge simply to stop. What examples do you have?

> **Reflect & Write:** Consider a time when you were 'in the zone', and time flew. After a long day, did you still feel wired? Ready to carry on and on. Wishing that you had all the time in the world to continue because you were buzzing? Bring those moments to your mind and write down a couple.

Of course, we experience the opposite too, when time drags. When I started secondary school, I remember the groan around the classroom as our timetable was revealed. Thursday mornings started with a double period of history – 75 minutes sitting still on hard wooden seats, fixed in position behind square desks with lids that lifted, and sufficiently separated from our neighbour to prevent playful distraction of one another. The teacher talking to the blackboard as we copied the chalk scribbles into our exercise books. At half time, the bell would go, our gaze was drawn to the window to see other students chatting, walking, skipping, across the playground to their next lesson – jealous of their five minutes of freedom. Finally, we were allowed to drag ourselves out of prison, energy depleted.

> **Reflect & Write:** What in your recent past has been energy draining?

These are the two extremes and indicate the full range of our energetic state, and most of the time, you will be somewhere between the two. So, let's consider 'most of the time': how would you describe the level of energy you bring to your life?

Reflect & Write: Take a brief audit of your average week. As a percentage, how much time do you spend in each of the energy zones?
1. Max Power
2. Energized
3. Neutral
4. Drained
5. Turned-off

Your goal over the remainder of this chapter is to set a plan to increase the time you spend in zones 1 and 2, eliminate zones 4 and 5, and be OK in neutral from time to time.

Low Energy Society

In his blog 'Why Working in Sprints Maximises Human Productivity'[49] Nils Salzgeber explains: *'We can't sprint 100% for more than 10-20 seconds. We can't concentrate for hours and hours on end.'*

Yet we kid ourselves that this is possible. Modern society rejects the need for rest with 'working lunches', holiday allowances carried over year after year and so on. We live in a low energy society where we are rarely fully charged and giving everything we have, and this is because we don't allow ourselves periods of total recovery.

We live in a world where we're never fully engaged or fully disengaged. Instead, we live in a thick mud of constant energy preservation.

At the other end of the spectrum, it is possible to exert too little energy. Doing nothing leads to lethargy that is difficult to shake. We perform at our best when we move between expending energy and intermittently renewing energy.

Maintaining the Car

Warren Buffett often tells great little stories to illustrate a profound point. In one of my favourites, he imagines a genie arriving to offer him a brand new, top of the range car of his dreams. With one catch – it is the only car he will ever receive, and therefore it has to last his entire lifetime. He then talks about how he'd polish the car, store it in a garage, check the oil, fix scratches, and read the manual many times over. That if he didn't do this, 10 years down the line his only car would be wrecked.

Now imagine that he isn't talking about a car, he's talking about his mind and his body. We get just one of each to last a lifetime, and if we don't take great care of them every day, then 10 years down the line one of them will be wrecked.

Cars need oil, petrol, water and coolant all of the time in order to operate. Over time the car engine consumes them, and they need to be refilled. You too have four energy needs which need to be present all of the time, all of which get consumed, and all need replacing. But unlike the car, they aren't separated into different tanks, replenishing one has the immediate effect of replenishing the others. Allow one to run dry, and all of them do.

The four energy dimensions introduced by Jim Loehr and Tony Schwartz in their outstanding book, *The Power of Full Engagement*[50] are:

- **Physical:** Does your body function well? Do you nourish it with the right food and plenty of water? Does it get a full night's sleep? Do you exercise it?
- **Emotional:** What is your default emotional state? Do you typically feel positive or negative emotions? How easily do you bounce back from feeling low?
- **Mental:** Can you remain engaged in something for long periods? Is your brain regularly stretched, and sufficiently rested?
- **Spiritual:** Are your actions driven by a strong sense of purpose? Do you feel motivated to do what you do?

Driving in the most fuel-efficient manner requires a constant speed of 55mph. No accelerating, no braking. Despite this, at some point, the fuel tank runs dry, and your journey ends, not because you reached your destination, but because you ran out of fuel.

Living life at a constant moderate speed lacks the exhilaration of adventure and challenge, nor does it allow for pauses to simply be content. And at some point, you run out of fuel. You half recharge at the weekend, you crave an annual holiday, you live life in the slow lane.

Instead, you want to be able to hit top gear when the road is clear and take a break when there's a scenic picnic spot. You need to 'oscillate'; spend and renew energy. Balance stress and recovery. Develop a sustainable rhythm of energy expenditure and renewal in all four energy dimensions.

The goal is to develop habits that work rhythmically, so for about 90 minutes you are in high-performance mode: your alertness, concentration, creativity, emotional resilience, and mental stamina are all at the top of their game. Then, for about 20 minutes, your body needs time to rest and renew its energy stores. We need to either fully engage or strategically disengage.

Do you ever completely relax? Do you ever fully disengage from what you're doing during the day? Do you take frequent breaks? Do you ever fully concentrate and give 100 per cent to a given task? Are you so busy sawing that you forget to sharpen the saw?

MAPPING YOUR ENERGY
Energy Awareness
What provides you with energy is different for all of us. As we established in Chapter 1, we are unique. We also know that before embarking on a journey, we need to know our destination and our start point. The goal is to maximize our time in energy zones 1 and 2, but where are you starting from?

Previously you estimated how much time you spent in each energy zone; now let's get more forensic about what causes your energy to rise and fall across all the four dimensions.

For each statement below, choose yes (Y), disagree (N), or neither (?):

	Y	?	N
Physical: I consistently sleep well, and wake refreshed			
Physical: I have a balanced diet and don't skip meals			
Physical: I exercise sufficiently to get out of breath three times per week			
Emotional: I spend sufficient high-quality time with people I care about			
Emotional: I allow myself time to enjoy hobbies			
Emotional: I regularly reflect on the good things in my life			
Mental: I can push away distractions to concentrate on important tasks			
Mental: I take time to plan rather than getting caught up in a whirlwind of busyness			
Mental: At weekends, in evenings, and on holidays I can fully switch off from work			
Spiritual: I know what is important to me and prioritize my time accordingly			
Spiritual: I spend most of my time doing things that I am good at and enjoy			
Spiritual: I make a positive impact on the world			

For every 'yes' score +1, for every 'no' score -1. What is your overall energy score? If you score over 4, while there may be areas to improve, your lifestyle is supporting sustainable levels of energy. Between -3 and +3, you're likely to experience fluctuations in energy levels, and -4 or less, oh dear, the batteries are empty most of the time.

But don't despair. We have a growth mindset. You're

measuring your past, and where you are today is a result of the habits of the past. If you've been living a life with a dead battery, just imagine what you are capable of in the future when you've learnt the skills of energy management.

Energy Equation

The previous two exercises have grown your energy self-awareness, so what actions now feel sensible? To grow the amount of positive energy you are feeling, the equation is simple, do more of the things that bring you energy, and less of the things that don't.

Reflect & Write: What will you do more of? What will you do less of?

THE FOUR SOURCES OF ENERGY

We have briefly introduced the four dimensions of energy, and you have just run a simple self-assessment; in this section, we will explore each dimension in greater detail and establish how you can grow your energy. Remember that each dimension feeds off the others; your goal is to optimize the whole system.

It's entirely down to you, squarely in box 2. Supremely important, but rarely of such burning urgency that your panic monster kicks into gear. External interferences are strong, so you must be stronger. It may feel selfish to spend time boosting your own energy, but if you don't have it, then you can't bring it others, and you're letting everyone down.

Next time you take a flight, listen carefully to the safety demonstration:

'Oxygen and air pressure are always being monitored.

*In the event of a decompression, an oxygen mask will automatically appear in front of you. To start the flow of oxygen, pull the mask towards you. Place it firmly over your nose and mouth, secure the elastic band behind your head, and breathe normally. Although the bag doesn't inflate, oxygen is flowing to the mask. If you are travelling with a child or someone who requires assistance, **secure your mask first**, and then assist the other person'.*[51]

The underlined words are critically important. If you can't breathe, then you are unable to help others.

If you are burnt out, tired, and running on empty, you can't help others (particularly if serving others is the primary cause of the energy deficit). Right now, you must bring an intention to constantly nourish your energy and take responsibility for it.

PHYSICAL ENERGY

The genie in Warren Buffet's story gave him one car for life. The genie has given you this remarkable contraption called a 'body', and you get just one of them. By maintaining it daily, you dramatically increase the performance that it is capable of and increase the probability that it will serve you well into old age. Failure to maintain it well leads to a breakdown, and it gets sick. Servicing your body is straightforward; it simply needs sleep, nutrition and exercise.

Sleep[52]

Sleep is the foundation of physical energy, and a true panacea: a remedy for almost all difficulties. It is the single biggest influence on our health, happiness and success. A full night of high-quality sleep refreshes the immune system, moderates appetite, increases the ability to learn, processes memories, establishes emotional balance, boosts confidence, enhances willpower and ambition, and enhances social interactions. Even minimal amounts of sleep deprivation wreak havoc with your ability to focus and concentrate.

Studies show that 95 per cent of us need seven to eight hours of sleep,[53] but it's one of the first behaviours we cut to get more done so in reality two-thirds of adults in developed nations fall short of this ideal.[54]

Reflect & Write: How about you? What is the quality of your sleep like?

Your body has two processes for telling you when to sleep: increasing levels of melatonin caused by your circadian rhythm that tells the brain whether it is day or night; and increasing levels of the hormone adenosine which causes increased levels of 'sleepiness' the longer you've been awake.

Artificial light (and particularly light emitted from screens) reduces the release of melatonin; stimulants like caffeine interfere with how your brain receives 'sleepiness' messages for up to six hours and alcohol-induced sleep has significantly lower quality.

To improve your sleep quality:

- Stick to a schedule: Going to bed and rising at the same time each day.
- Establish a pre-bedtime routine: In the half-hour before bed, do the same things in the same order. This programmes the body ready for rest.
- Avoid caffeine at least six hours before bed; alcohol, and heavy meals or intensive exercise less than two hours before bed.
- Turn off all screens at least half an hour before bed.

Nutrition

A Google search for 'healthy eating' returns 931 million results in half-a-second; all of them with something slightly different to offer, and many of them contradictory. Keeping things straightforward as we focus on nutrition purely through an energy lens: it's all about glucose. The body and the brain are powered by glucose and require a steady supply.

I was introduced to the term 'hangry' recently, and it's a pretty accurate description of both the cause and the symptom of my mood changes. My wife often diagnoses it better than I do, particularly if we're out somewhere for the day. If I make an uncharacteristic negative comment, she asks if I'm hungry.

The answer is usually 'yes!' There is a direct link between my mood and my blood-sugar level. You may not experience such an obvious emotional swing, but you will certainly experience a loss of energy if you're short of glucose.

The short-term fix is to get a hit of sugar. Reach for a cookie. But you've heard of the sugar crash: when you eat too much sugar, your body produces insulin very quickly, causing a delayed deficit in glucose levels.

To manage your blood-sugar level, follow these simple tips:

- Eat breakfast. It is the most important meal of the day because it gets your blood sugar levels up and kickstarts the body's metabolic functions.
- Eat something at least every three hours.
- Avoid sugar and simple carbohydrates; protein and complex carbohydrates are much better.

Alongside glucose, the other main short-term impact on

energy is hydration. Water makes up 68 per cent of our body weight, and 73 per cent of the brain.[55] When you're dehydrated your mood shifts, your brain has to work harder to function, and your muscles become fatigued. By the time you're feeling thirsty you're already dehydrated. Keep sipping sufficient water throughout the day. An easy check that you're drinking enough is to check the colour of urine; it should be a pale clear colour.

Reflect & Write: Complete this sentence: 'I can better manage my blood sugar throughout the day by...'

Exercise

You already know that exercise is good for you, and you know why. Regular exercise leads to a dramatic increase in overall physical energy, and many will tell you it's also their secret weapon in developing emotional and mental wellbeing.

In the past, when you have exercised, you may have said: 'I feel so much better because of it.' Yet it is THE classic case of short-term pain for long-term gain. The procrastination monkey loves this topic and is a master at playing the game. Here's the evidence that the chimp is winning in the UK:[56]

Only 13 per cent exercise regularly, 34 per cent with some regularity, 16 per cent seldom exercise and a whopping 37 per cent never exercise.

Regular exercise: increases mental alertness, energy and mood,[57] increases self-esteem,[58] reduces stress and anxiety, [59] and positively impacts mental health.[60]

Reflect & Write: Are you in the 13 per cent that takes this seriously? If not, what could you begin to do to benefit from the magic of exercise?

Please note, you should build up the level of exercise you take slowly. Overstretching yourself can lead to injury, stepping things up nice and slowly is more motivating and easier to stick to long term. Any type of movement is better than none, so if you're in the 37 per cent who never exercise, start simply by introducing a reason to walk regularly (e.g. getting off the bus a stop earlier, or avoiding escalators and elevators to take the stairs).

MENTAL ENERGY

Your mental energy is your ability to focus on what you want, when you want, and for however long you want. Have you ever worked on a task during the afternoon or evening that took an hour or more, that you know you could have completed in 10 minutes? It is due to mental fatigue.

When we lack mental energy, we are not only making poor use of our time, but our ability to make rational decisions is compromised because we take the easy option rather than the right option. Take a look at the serious, life-changing effect of low brain energy (caused by low glucose level) in a case study examined by Daniel Kahneman,[61] of parole judges in Israel.

A panel of judges spends an average of six minutes reviewing the merits of individual parole cases, all day, every day. The 'safe' option is to refuse parole, the riskier option is to approve the early release of a prisoner, and this happens in 35 per cent of cases. But what is most interesting is when the ratio of approvals versus rejections is plotted against the time of the day the decision is taken. Kahneman found that directly after food breaks the approval rate was 65 per cent and that over the following two hours it steadily dropped to close to zero.

Whether a prisoner is released on parole has less to do with the merits of their case, and more to do with whether judges have high or low mental energy.

Mental Recovery: Taking Breaks

In 2014, the social networking company, The Draugiem Group, used a time-tracking productivity app to study what habits set their most productive employees apart from the rest. Surprisingly, the top 10 per cent of employees with the highest productivity didn't put in longer hours than anyone else – often they didn't even work eight-hour days. Instead, the key to their productivity was that for every 52 minutes of focused work, they took a 17-minute break.[62]

I bet when you're a facing deadline that the last thing that you do is plan breaks every hour. Yet our brains can't bring devoted attention to a single task for much more than 60 to 90 minutes. 'Oh yes I can, I can do a full eight-hour shift without a break.' Yes, you can be all there in body, in front of your screen for eight solid hours, but is your attention there the whole time. The answer is a categorical NO!

Humans can't multitask because we're biologically hardwired to undertake tasks sequentially and can't perform two cognitive tasks at the same time. To say that our attention is divided is equally untrue – at a given moment we can't consciously place 50 per cent of attention on one topic (for example a webinar), and the remaining 50 per cent on a second topic (for example writing emails) – what is actually happening is that you are toggling between giving 100 per cent attention briefly to topic one, and then 100 per cent attention briefly to topic two. Because it takes time to get the brain fully immersed in a topic, when attempting two things at once, you never bring all of your mental capacity to either.

The key to making the most of your mental energy is to bring your full undivided, uninterrupted attention to a single task for between 50 and 90 minutes, and then to rest fully, for between 5 and 20 minutes. When you're focussed, it means no pop-up notifications, no dings or rings on your phone, nobody entering your workspace, no desk tidying, no tea making or Google browsing. You are fully in the zone. When you're resting you physically leave your workspace and do something completely different.

After the break, not only do you come back with greater cognitive energy (a glucose level increase and a glass of water), you will often come back with new answers to questions that you'd been struggling with before the break. This is because your brain's computing capacity has been temporarily diverted from working logically, and instead has been giving space for unconscious connections to be made. Have you ever had your best ideas when you've been most relaxed? Sure you have! Daydreaming on the commute or in the shower, when walking or in the middle of the night. It turns out you get more done when you deliberately temporarily switch off.

Reflect & Write: What is your working rhythm like? How can you build in periods of full focus, followed by planned downtime?

Effort Differences

The rate at which your mental energy is consumed is determined by how challenging the thinking is.

What is the capital of France? What comes next, spring, summer, autumn? What is 2+2? Not so challenging, right? Psychologists would say these types of questions activate your 'system 1' mode of thinking, and Daniel Kahneman describes this mode of thinking as: *'operating automatically and quickly, with little or no effort and no sense of voluntary control'.*[63]

Now, look at the following problem: What is 17 x 24?

As the solution probably isn't intuitive, system 1 can't help you. This problem requires your 'system 2' mode of thinking: an allocation of computational power to this specific problem for a concentrated time.

Certain activities simply require system 1 and therefore, don't consume mental energy. While others require healthy doses of computational power to be available. When you're fresh, such activities may only take you 10 minutes, but late at night when your mental energy is low, it can take a full hour.

Remember back to the last chapter, where you were scheduling your activities. The box 2 activities need to come first, not simply because you may not get around to them if they don't, but because these are the most important and often most complex tasks that require system 2 at its freshest.

When planning your day, and even your week, consider which activities are your most challenging and put these into your schedule when you expect to have the most available mental energy. Equally, allocate routine work to your low energy moments.

Building Mental Capacity

How far you can run non-stop is primarily related to how far you ran before. It's a matter of training. How long you can exert brainpower is related to how long you typically exert brainpower. The brain gets sharper the more it's used, and you can build mental capacity in just the same way as building physical capacity – with practice. But for many, the formal training programme ends on the day of graduation from school.

Continual education and mind expansion are vital to developing new mental muscles and to protect us from decline as we age. To keep the brain fresh, we need to feed it intriguing dishes. The greatest minds in science, business, politics, the arts and education explore subjects outside their field in great depth, think analytically and critically express themselves. The busiest of business leaders find space for continuing education, they read broadly, get exposed to different points of view, and constantly challenge their assumptions about the world.

How do you keep your mind fresh? Do you live in an echo-chamber, constantly experiencing the same points of view? Or do you actively seek diverse opinions? What fields are you interested in, and how do you deepen your understanding of them?

Reflect & Write: 'To keep expanding my mind I will... '

SPIRITUAL ENERGY

Viktor E. Frankl, a Viennese doctor and psychiatrist, survived four Nazi death and labour camps during World War II, to write his memoir *Man's Search for Meaning*[64] in nine days in 1946. Through it, he teaches that everyone must find his or her unique meaning and purpose in life and fulfil it. This is the source of what we call 'spiritual energy'.

Life in the labour camps showed Frankl that men who could hold onto even a small sense of purpose found that it helped them survive. Those who ceased to believe in tomorrow didn't. In February 1945, a friend of Frankl's dreamed that the camp would be liberated on March 30.

On March 29, amid reports that Allied advances had slowed and wouldn't reach the camp by that date, the man fell into a deep fever and died the next day. Typhus appeared to be the cause, but Frankl knew his friend's loss of belief in his future killed him. Life becomes meaningless when we have nothing to strive for.

Immense spiritual energy comes from trying to reach a goal with profound personal meaning. Where there is an absence of meaning, there exists a sense of emptiness, manifesting as boredom (even while busy). If there is no clear 'why' to your doing an activity, then energy will be lacking. If there is a deep 'why', then you'll feel like you can scale mountains and push through seemingly impossible roadblocks.

Spiritual Energy is the most powerful source of motivation, perseverance and direction.

How do you get it? You just need two things. First, to be deeply connected with your sense of purpose in life (knowing that this sense of purpose may evolve as you live it). Second, aligning your priorities so that you feel like you are journeying towards it.

It may be some time since you started working through this book, so let's spend a moment revisiting the work that you have already done to expand your spiritual energy.

Reflect & Write: On page 8, you identified your core values and how fully you were living them. How are you doing now? Are there any changes that you would like to make so that you can live them even more fully?

Reflect & Write: On page 17 we introduced the metaphor of the keel of the boat to represent your deep connection to your sense of purpose, and later (page 117) you thought about the guiding North Star – what is yours? Things may have changed since then, so have a go now at writing your purpose statement as it stands today.

When setting your top priority goals, you worked to establish the 'why' for each of them (page 121). Are these goals still your most important ones? And when you read through the 'whys' are they powerfully motivating?

Finally, when considering how you plan your time, does your diary now include sufficient box 2 (page 167) time so that you feel you're on the journey towards your purpose (and the big rocks on page 162) or is your diary full of sand?

Reflect & Write: Complete this sentence: 'If I am not giving sufficient time to feel like I'm making progress, I will create more box 2 time by...'

There is nothing new to add. No new theories or actions. This book is built around helping you to grow your spiritual energy. If you don't feel you're there yet, as though your sense of purpose is still a two out of 10, be OK with that. Keep reflecting on the questions in this section, and it will come – sometimes in a 'wow, that's it' flash, and sometimes as a slow evolution over many years, shaped by how your life evolves. So just leave the question sitting in your subconscious and be confident that an answer will emerge whenever it is supposed to.

SOCIAL/EMOTIONAL ENERGY

In Chapter 3, we explored how you can manage your emotional state. While acknowledging that the full range of human emotions is necessary and valuable, we also know that some emotions build energy while others drain them. If life is represented by a carousel of emotions, we'd rather be up more than we're down.

When we feel safe, valued, respected and appreciated we have the capacity for greater self-confidence, empathy and sociability, which in turn feeds a positive cycle.

Emotional Audit

Back on page 52, we introduced a list of different emotions, which we can categorize as positive or negative; energy giving or energy draining. When contemplating how you're feeling now, you may choose something from the positive list, or the negative list, or perhaps simply somewhere in the middle – neither noticeably positive nor negative. If you had been tracking your emotional state over the past few months, what percentage of your time would you spend in each of the following zones?

Negative and Energy Draining	Neutral	Positive and Energy Building
Negative and forceful: Anger, annoyance, contempt, disgust, irritation		**Positive and lively:** Amusement, delight, elation, excitement, happiness, joy, pleasure
Negative and not in control: Anxiety, embarrassment, fear, helplessness, powerlessness, worry		**Caring:** Affection, empathy, friendliness, love
Negative thoughts: Pride, doubt, envy, frustration, guilt, shame		**Positive thoughts:** Courage, hope, humility, satisfaction, trust
Agitation: Stress, shock, tension		**Reactive:** Interest, politeness, surprise
%	%	%

Experiencing positive emotional energy is as simple as spending more time on the right-hand side of the table, and less on the left-hand side. Whatever your current reality, you can shift things if you're willing to make the first move.

Quite unfairly however, to experience positive emotions, we sometimes have to risk some of the negative ones. When showing affection for others, we risk embarrassment. When displaying courage, we're more open to doubt; hope can turn to despair; trust can turn to hurt.

There is typically a large middle ground, and this could be OK. The question for you *is*, is it OK? Is the amount of time you spend not experiencing much emotionally, the right amount of time? The goal isn't only to experience positive emotions; this would be a strange existence and a completely unrealistic one. What you're seeking is a good balance, so you can bring energy to our daily life.

Social Energy

Positive relationships build emotional energy. Genuine friendships are critical, as is the capacity to love and be loved. Humans are inherently social animals, and the highlights of our lives are typically those moments we share with other people.

Before my last trip to Singapore, a friend who knows the country well wrote down a list of the best things to do there. It included spending sunset at a bar at the 2.5-acre garden perched at the top of the 57-storey Marina Bay Sands Hotel, with 360-degree views over the city. Sounds idyllic, right? Until I pictured being alone, surrounded by people who weren't. Then it felt like hell. I'd miss my wife terribly.

Time spent with loved ones or nurturing friendships is one of life's necessities. Yet often, this time gets squeezed out.

Reflect & Write: How about for you? When you reflect on the time that you spend with the people who bring you joy, is there enough of it?

Equally, some relationships are the cause of our suffering. We all need to feel appreciated and respected, and when we don't, we are emotionally vulnerable. Feeling safe is the second level of Maslow's hierarchy of needs[65] (second only to physiological needs such as food and water), and until we feel safe, we are unable to develop motivation for more satisfying activities. Relationships have a hugely significant impact on our lives, so we'll be putting them squarely in the spotlight in the next chapter.

Intrinsic Emotional Energy

While acknowledging that other people and external events can impact our emotional state, the work we did in Chapter 3 developed your ability to maintain emotional balance regardless of extrinsic factors. Intrinsic emotional security comes from within. If you value, appreciate and respect yourself, then the impact of others is lessened. You will have the strength to be authentic, open, vulnerable and trusting.

You've been working on this topic since Chapter 1, and it's all wrapped up in the single concept of self-regard. It's about having deep inner belief in yourself. We'll conclude this book by drawing together all the strands that you've been working on – building your confidence that you are OK exactly as you are, AND that allowing yourself to be even more you is the key to life fulfilment. When you live a life that is congruent with your deepest values and in line with your sense of purpose, then you build your intrinsic protective blanket.

Creating Positive Emotional Moments

The more positive emotions you're regularly feeling, the more emotional energy you'll have and the higher the level of your performance. Many believe that success comes before happiness, but in reality, evidence shows that it works the other way around. Happy people are more successful. Would you benefit from devoting more time to seeking pleasurable emotions? I've never met anyone that says 'no'. So assuming your answer is 'yes', what would you like to feel more of, and how will you do it?

Reflect & Write: Select five words from the list of positive emotions on page 52 that you'd like to experience more often. Then for each word, go into 'divergent thinking mode' and generate a long list of all the things which could cause you to feel that way. Get a blank page and go wild, get creative and fill it with anything that comes to mind, the goal is to have lots of options you can pick from later.

Reflect & Write: Now it is time for 'convergent thinking mode'. Select what you intend to do.

RESILIENCE

What causes you to give up on something?

Were you too physically exhausted to continue? Or burnt out so your brain could no longer function effectively? Or were you questioning why it was worth the effort? Or perhaps feeling emotionally drained?

You quit because you ran out of one of the sources of energy. To grow resilience, you need to develop positive energy management habits.

Stretch and Renewal

Currently, I don't have the physical energy to run a half-marathon. In four months, I need to run one as the final leg of a half-Ironman competition. To build my capacity, I need to do two things. To build endurance, my training programme needs to be consistently stretching. Currently, 10km is pretty comfortable, 14km is getting tougher. When I hit the 15th and 16th kilometres, it hurts. But these are the only kilometres that really count. All the others just took me to the point where the training began to have an impact. Last year I pushed hard in my training. Too hard. I got injured because I didn't do the second thing that is required to build my capacity, which is to recover effectively between training sessions.

By following the rules of energy development, stretch and renewal, I will get to the point where a half-marathon feels easy. I will have built my capacity.

We can take this sporting metaphor and apply it to all four energy dimensions. If you're not actively stretching yourself, you won't grow your capacity, and in fact, as you age, your capacity will diminish. If you're not creating space for recovery you're more likely to become tired, burnt out, injured or sick.

To grow your energy in each dimension do you need more stretch, more recovery or both?

Physical energy	more stretch / more recovery / both
Spiritual energy	more stretch / more recovery / both
Mental energy	more stretch / more recovery / both
Emotional energy	more stretch / more recovery / both

Energizing Lifestyle

As you worked through this chapter, you'll have noted down some actions that you could take to increase your energy in each of the four dimensions. These actions usually require you to break an old habit and therefore require willpower. As we established back in Chapter 2, you have a finite reserve of willpower, and it consumes energy to exert it.

Habits are the key to sustainability.

Reflect & Write: What energy-enhancing habits would you like to develop?

Back on page 35, you learnt how to foster positive habits. Run the list above through the same process and enjoy greater energy in your life.

Concluding Thoughts

Resilience is connected with energy, and building capacity requires cyclic shifts between stretch and renewal in all four energy dimensions. The four dimensions work symbiotically – building one builds them all, lowering one lowers them all.

Two key elements to emotional energy are the quality of your relationships with others, and the quality of the relationship with yourself. These are the topics for the final chapters.

CHAPTER 8
POSITIVE RELATIONSHIPS

Your emotional state is largely related to the nature of your relationships with the people you spend the most time with. If they are nurturing and respectful, you experience satisfaction, self-confidence and happiness. If they are critical and disrespectful, you experience sadness and low self-esteem.

William James says, 'the deepest principle in human nature is the craving to be appreciated', and Dale Carnegie[66] adds 'the rare individual who can honestly satisfy this heart hunger will hold people in the palm of his hand'.

This chapter marks a subtle but very important departure from previous sections. Everything we have discussed before this, you have the potential to control. You can't control another person – but as you will see, you can choose how you show up in a relationship, and this will influence your emotional state.

YOUR RELATIONSHIP RESERVOIR
Start by taking an audit of the people who you share your life with. Do they fill your emotional reservoir, or deplete

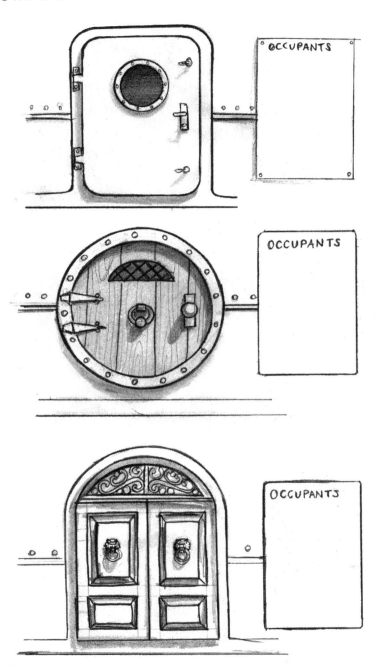

it? How can you increase the inflow of energy from those people who nourish you? How can you plug the drains of those that sap your enjoyment?

Who Is in Your Life?

You are sailing through life on a cruise ship, and you share it with a whole host of characters. Each room represents a different aspect of your life; some people don't move between rooms, some do. Let's give a name to each room and list the people that you can find there. Examples of room titles are work, family, neighbours, old friends, gym mates, fellow gamers, etc.

Reflect & Write: Look at the illustration on the previous page and give each door a name, and then list the people who you can meet behind it.

Your life satisfaction right now is largely due to the people you wrote down on your lists. This is who you spend your time with. These are the people who you want to be appreciated by. When you enter a room and spend time there, do you come out uplifted, or drained? Perhaps it depends who specifically is in the room.

So, who is it that builds you up and makes you feel good? Put a '+' next to their name. Who leaves you feeling worse? Put a '–' next to their name.

How does it feel to 'rate' people? You're judgemental because I am asking you to be. But let's be clear about what you are rating. The symbol that you have put next to a name isn't a judgement of that person. It is a judgement of the nature of your relationship with them – it is your feelings that you have been rating. How you feel is down to you. Sure, behaviours of others will trigger an emotional reaction, and from time to time you will say 'they make me feel... '

But you can't control them, and they can't control you. You can influence them, and they can influence you. In this chapter, we'll explore how you can create a separation between the behaviour of someone else and how you feel; and on the flip side, how you can behave so that others would attach a + symbol to your name.

Everyone is Unique and Imperfect

By this point, you'll have noticed that you are not perfect, and you know you never will be. You've been socially conditioned. You have bad habits that are hard to shake. You have down days and up days. Your emotions get triggered by external events. You have a unique set of values and beliefs. In fact, you're wonderfully, magically unique, and all those lumps and bumps and idiosyncrasies make you YOU. And this is what makes the human race so frustratingly amazing.

And it's not just you. EVERYONE is unique. They may say they're fine, but often this is not true. Remember the 'Myth of Okayness' – if you really ask, and they really trust you, then you will find that everyone is carrying with them some sense that, in some way, they are not OK; and that in some way, they too are struggling. So, let's quieten the voice of judgement. Their behaviour isn't because of you, at its root is something about themselves.

But this is hard because evolution has planted a trick inside us. We all pattern match and make assumptions about people based on our past experiences. A series of experiments by Princeton psychologists Janine Willis and Alexander Todorov[67] reveal that all it takes is a tenth of a second to form an impression of a stranger from their face. Then, because subconsciously we're then looking for evidence that our initial assessment was right – longer exposure doesn't significantly alter those first impressions, they simply boost confidence in the initial judgement.

One of the traits we judge in the blink of an eye is whether we trust the other person or not, and trust is at the foundation of good relationships. Take a look at the characters below, who are you most likely to trust and why?

No one is the same as you, and the greater the differences appear to be the more we feel uncomfortable. When we enter a room of strangers, we are drawn to people we perceive to be similar to ourselves – we have to bring conscious effort to want to get to know the people who are different. You have to bring conscious effort to re-see people, with fresh eyes, to honour and respect their differences and their right to believe, value, and behave differently to you. Sometimes you will remember to do this, and often, you won't.

It's the same for others too. They formed a first impression about you, their subconscious is pattern matching, and it takes time for them to reform an opinion as they get to know the real you.

When you see another person for who they really are, beyond their clothing and projected persona, you'll find the universal truth that everyone, at some point, has struggled with every topic covered in this book. You will find that we are more alike than you have ever realised. As a species, we're a family of human beings with common desires and motives; as individuals, we are full of wonderful idiosyncrasies. Your ability to hold both truths in your mind is the key to believing you can enjoy wonderful relationships with anyone that you meet.

Reflect & Write Which 10 people do you spend the most time with and do they boost your emotional energy, or do they drain it? Plot their names on a mood line.

EMOTIONAL DRAINS ←   NEUTRAL   EMOTIONAL BOOST →

Stepping back to take in the whole picture; your emotional state is a reflection of the weight on the line. If you have more weight on the right, you are likely to feel good. More weight on the left, and you are likely to feel drained. The goal, therefore, is to shift the weight to the right. Of course, it would be wonderful to simply spend all of your time with people who quite naturally boost your emotional energy, but things aren't always that straightforward. You need to find ways to both reduce the emotional drain of the relationships that aren't currently working, while also maximising the energy boost that you get from naturally positive relationships.

Never Too Much of a Good Thing

Reflect & Write: Who brings out the best in you? Who makes you feel good? Select five people who boost your emotional energy, and then be precise about what positive emotions they invoke in you. (Here's a reminder of some positive emotional states: amusement, delight, elation, excitement, happiness, joy, pleasure, affection, empathy, friendliness, love, courage, hope, humility, satisfaction, trust, calmness, contentment, relaxation, relief, and serenity.)

Reflect & Write: The relationship is likely reciprocal – you boost their emotional energy in some way. So, what do you do for them? Think of each person in turn – how do you make them feel good?

These relationships are entirely positive for both of you, and the effect of spending time together boosts your entire system. With these people, you genuinely can't have too much of a good thing. So, let's go for 10 per cent more.

This can either be 10 per cent more time in total or bringing 10 per cent more quality to the time that you do have together. Quality comes from the level of attention that you both bring to one another. I spend a lot of time with my wife, and during the vast majority of that time, our focus is on our children. Drinking a coffee while sitting down one-on-one with no phones, or kids, or to-do lists, just once per day would increase the quality of our connection by at least 10 per cent.

Reflect & Write: What can you do to increase the quality or quantity of connection that you have with your top five energy boosters?

Water the Flowers, Not the Weeds

When you take a watering can to the garden, you deliberately pour the water on the flowers that you want to flourish. This is what you're doing in the exercise above: considering which relationships you want to nurture and blossom, and therefore being deliberate about where you place your focus.

Weeds grow in your garden too: they suck nutrients from the ground, stunt the growth of the flowers, and take up space and light. You don't take your watering can and pour water on them. In life, some individuals take your light and suck your nutrients, so why feed them with your attention and emotional energy?

Reflect & Write: Who drains your energy, what weeds are you watering? Bring them into your mind and write down how it feels to be thinking about them now.

Stepping back and looking at what you have written in the box above, has your style of writing changed from the previous exercises? How hard you pressed on the page? The size of the lettering? Exclamation marks? Formation of letters?

You'll probably find the inner emotions come straight through you, down your arm and out of your pen. Your inner state of mind has affected your behaviour – in this instance, it's just how you wrote, and only you can notice the subtle difference. This person isn't with you now, has done nothing in the last five minutes to trigger your change in behaviour, and yet your behaviour is altered simply by your memory of them.

Later in the chapter, we'll look at how you can alter your relationships with 'difficult' people. For now. though, notice which relationships you're watering. Does most of your attention go to those people who build you up? Or do you water the weeds by allowing uncomfortable memories to constantly resurface and affect your state of mind?

If you're like many people, you'll spend a huge amount of time replaying bad situations, spinning them this way and that. Sometimes at night. Sometimes all night! Round and round they go, causing negative moods. Causing you not to see the flowers at all. All your water is falling on the weeds. If you explained it to someone else, you'd fear being judged as petty, and told to 'just get over it'. But you can't. It eats away at you. When this happens to me I find the only solution is to give it my full attention for a short period of time. I take a blank sheet of paper and write down all the thoughts that come into my head, in whatever order they happen to come out. I'm not attempting to get to a solution or to write a coherent report, I'm just letting my hand flow as fast as the thoughts emerge.

You'll have a go at this in a minute, the trick isn't to be writer and editor at the same time – your hand is just the transcriber of the voice inside your head.

Reflect & Write: Choose the biggest weed in your life, the one that gets the inner emotions boiling, and simply begin to transcribe what comes up.

You started off fast, right, and then things slowed, and then there was a burst of speed as another thing came up. Then you paused. Then you said 'AND ANOTHER THING...' And eventually, nothing new came up. Everything that has been spinning around your mind is on the page. You can take a step back and say, 'Yes, that's it.'

When you look at the page, you observe the outpouring of your 'chimp mind'. It's fuelled by emotion. I find that when these thoughts have literally come straight out of my head and are looking back at me from the page I can find some emotional separation. It's as though the rational human within me can observe the chimp as separate from myself, and the chimp settles down, knowing it has been fully heard and respected.

Nothing externally is fixed, of course. But you're laying the groundwork for the fixing to begin by acknowledging the emotion, but not being controlled by it. This leads us beautifully into the next section as we'll see that at times throughout our life, our childish emotions take over and control our behaviour and this is true for your 'difficult' people too.

WHEN THERE'S NO RESPECT

Some relationships are lop-sided; one person feeling inferior to another in certain ways, and therefore somehow being dependent on the other.

You can observe this dynamic in all childhood relationships; we all can play the superior or inferior partner, and we can all be triggered into either role throughout our adult life. By using the lens of transactional analysis,[68] we'll deconstruct what's happening and learn how to rebalance things so that there is mutual respect.

Transactional Analysis

When you were born, what could you do? Practically nothing! You were completely dependent on grown-ups to give you nourishment and safety and love. At this point in life, you had no language to explain things rationally – you simply had feelings. The grown-ups did something, and you felt an emotion, and it caused you to cry or scream or smile or giggle.

Eric Berne would call this a transaction: one person did something, and a second person had a reaction. His 1964 book, *Games People Play*[69] coded these transactions, and we'll be borrowing from his work and terminology to dig a little deeper into what causes a lack of respect in some relationships.

Berne talks about our ability to transact from one of three states throughout our life: the child, the parent and the adult. Furthermore, he explains how one state naturally triggers a corresponding state in the other person.

First, let's explore the child state. As infants, we are small, helpless and dependent. We have internal reactions to external events, and this emotional body of data remains with us for life. We experience grown-ups (in Berne's language – 'Parents'), and they appear superior to us in every way. Their appraisals of us go in unfiltered, we're not equipped to judge them, so we form a picture of ourselves by how others react to us. All of this is unshakeable. Our child is with us every moment for the rest of our lives and can be triggered at any moment. Sometimes the child that gets triggered is our joyful, creative, imaginative, giggling child; and sometimes it is the criticized, judged, belittled, dependent child (like when someone points out that we're not acting like responsible adults).

As we grow up, we record all the behaviours, actions, say-ings and habits of the people around us. This forms the basis of the 'Parent State', which can be triggered within us throughout life. If you have siblings you may have received from them the words of your parents even when you were both children. My five-year-old son Wilbur now says to his 11-year old sister, 'Olive, you can't go on your phone until you've done your homework.' He's recorded the authorita-tive voice of his parents; tone, timing and all! You too can bring out your authoritative voice when it's required – the voice of superiority.

We'll come to the adult state later, but first, we'll explore the dynamics between two people, one of who is in the child state, and one in the parent state. In a moment I'll ask you to recall when you've experienced each state, but first a story to bring it to life.

It's 6:45 am on a Sunday in summer. Five-year-old Olive and I come downstairs to have breakfast. She goes to the fridge and pulls out a full bottle of water.

'What's that?' I ask

'My special water,' responds Olive.

'I can see that, but we don't drink bottled water, we drink water from the tap,'

'But it's my special water, Dad.'

'Look, sweetheart, it's sparkling water, you don't even like sparkling water,' I say, taking the bottle from her.

'No, Dad, it's mine,' says my slightly upset child.

'Look, darling,' I say, bending down to get close to her face, 'it says here SP, that's the start of the word 'Sparkling'. You don't like sparkling water.'

At this point she takes the bottle from my hand and moves to begin to open it, 'Dad, it's my special water.'

'There's water in the tap, here's a glass, now sit down,' I say authoritatively, retaking the bottle and firmly putting it back into the fridge.

Sometime later, with my inner voice still recounting the incident and souring my mood, my wife walks in. Goes to the fridge. Takes out the bottle of water. Hands it to Olive, 'Olive, you didn't tell Dad about your special water!'

In this scenario, I was in the critical superior parent state, causing Olive to be in the criticized inferior child state. I had given her no space or respect. If I had, I would have understood that the previous day, while out shopping, her mum had bought and finished a sparkling bottle of water. Wanting to 'be like Mum', Olive too had wanted to drink from a bottle. So they refilled it – put it in the fridge so it was perfectly cold, and agreed that 'first thing tomorrow morning, let Dad know that your special water is in the fridge'.

Reflect & Write: When (recently) have you been pushed into the small, dependent, criticized child position? When have you been in Olive's shoes? How does it feel?

Reflect & Write: How about when you were in my position, taking the superior parent position? In the moment, it might have felt powerful, but reflecting on it, knowing that you caused the other person to feel like a controlled, inferior child. How does it feel?

Neither are great places to be, right? And it's easy to see how, when one person takes the critical parent position, the other person naturally falls into the criticized child role. Many people complain of micromanagement – and this is the reason they feel they are being treated like a child; under-trusted, under-respected, and undervalued. It works the other way around too. By taking a dependent child position, the natural response is for the other person to become the parent. Let's take a look at the work scenario.

'Hey, Boss. I'm really struggling with this thing. I just can't do it, and I'm really worried that I'll mess things up.'

'OK. Give it to me, I'll do it, don't worry about it.'

The employee comes to the boss as a helpless, dependent child, and the boss's natural parental instincts kick in to take the pain away from their 'child'. But what have we now set up? This dynamic gets repeated – the employee doesn't tackle anything challenging, their self-confidence gets lower. The boss takes on more and more work that really should be delegated but can't for fear of stressing the employee. It's an unhealthy working relationship that serves neither party.

That's enough of the theory. Let's look at the relationships in your life through this parent-child lens.

When You Are the Child

Reflecting on the whole spectrum of relationships that you have – peers, colleagues, neighbours, family members, siblings, friends, lecturers, receptionists, boss, subordinates – with whom do you have a parent-child relationship where you are often in the child position? Look for relationships where the balance of power lies with the other person, or you look up to them; or where you are dependent in some way; or where they 'mother you'; or where you are taken 'under someone's wing'.

Some of these may feel nurturing and loving rather than oppressive and critical – but nevertheless, the dynamic isn't of mutual respect, one person is perceived by both of you as superior.

Reflect & Write: *'People who are 'parents' to my 'child' are...*

While some relationships are fixed with this dynamic, in other relationships, the situation dictates what role each of you take. When it comes to our social life, my wife is the boss. I am happy to defer all decision-making to her and I go where I'm told we're going. When it comes to where we spend our summer holiday as a family, the roles are reversed. Considering your most important relationship, can you identify situations where you play the role of the child (willingly or not!).

Reflect & Write: *'Situations when I am the child include...'*

When You Are the Parent

Who do you look after? Who needs you to function effectively? Who can't be trusted on their own? With whom do you feel you need to put on your 'bossy' hat?

Reflect & Write: Identify five people from any walk of your life and consider why you find yourself in the 'parent' position.

As you parent them more, do you find that they act more childishly? You can get caught in a loop that is serving neither of you and possibly allows resentment to simmer.

Habitual Positions

You play different positions at different moments, and with different people. But do you have a strong default position? I know my tendency is towards 'parenting' and very infrequently find myself in the child role. In the past, my parenting bias has resulted in feedback about a perception of superiority, arrogance or ego. If I am to have positive relationships, it's clearly something that I need to bring conscious attention to.

Reflect & Write: Can you spot strong habitual positions in others? Who in your network is a stereotypical 'parent' (likes to be in charge) or stereotypical 'child' (is dependent on others)?

Reflect & Write: What about you? Do you have a bias towards one or the other? Or perhaps there's a clear link between the situation and your role. Take some notes about your natural tendencies in different situations.

You'll notice how default children (who are dependent on others), would be attracted to a default parent (who likes to be in control), and vice-versa. Many marriages last for many years based on this principle. You may have heard phrases like 'she wears the trousers', or 'he's under the thumb', which describe 'parent'-'child' marriages, (and both of which sound very old fashioned and sexist).

The Effect of Hierarchy

You're at school or university with a group of peers about to embark on a team project as equals. Then one of you is nominated as the leader. In an instant, there is a hierarchy. The physiology of the leader instantly changes; the mind says, 'I am responsible' and the natural position to take is that of 'parent'. In the same instant, everyone else is transported to the 'child' state. They sit back in their chair, relax and wait for the leader to take charge.

This is damaging for everyone involved, and if it is allowed to deepen, then the team will not function effectively. The leader will become 'the boss', feeling the need to control and micromanage a collection of subordinates who feel belittled and under-valued.

Other circumstances automatically trigger the parent-child dynamic, including interviewer and interviewee; teacher and student; and in many cultures, we can add age, gender, and social class.

Parent-child dynamics are everywhere, and is the default setting in many circumstances, particularly in organizational hierarchies. But they are built on inequality and a lack of mutual respect.

Adult-to-Adult Relationships

Thankfully, relationships don't have to be parent-child. Eric Berne introduced a third position from which we can interact with people. He called this the 'adult state'. You know what an adult-to-adult relationship looks and feels like. In the earlier section 'never too much of a good thing' (page 225), you identified five people who boost your energy, and you boost theirs.

Reflect & Write: When you consider each of those people, what words come to mind that describes the relationship and how it feels?

When you are in the adult state, you are aware of the input available from your 'child' and your 'parent' and can bring rational thought to your actions. When the other person is also in the adult state, this feels easy because there is mutual respect and a sense of equality.

Behaving Like an Adult

If you're locked in a parent-child dynamic, how do you shift it to adult-adult? Berne's book is called *Games People Play*, and the goal of the game he refers to is to maintain the current stable (if ineffective) relationship. People have grown up knowing how to play their game, without knowing they were playing one at all. It is built into the fabric of our culture. How you break the game is to change the rules. If you don't feed the child, they learn how to feed themselves. If you don't depend on the parent, they lose the ability to control you.

You change the rules by always playing from the adult position, regardless of which position the other person interacts with you from. Because you break the rules, the other person can't continue to be an adult or child. After some resistance (because they've got deeply ingrained habits), their only option is to meet you in the adult space. If you find yourself in the child space, your emotions are controlling you. It's time to use the techniques that you learnt and developed in Chapter 3 for managing your internal state.

If you find yourself acting like a parent, ask yourself

how you can decrease the perceived dependence of the other person. Is the root cause because you have an overcontrolling tendency, or because the other person has a feeling of inferiority? What would happen if you showed greater faith in their potential? The secret is contained in Chapter 2 – believe they can have a growth mindset, and it's your job to help them to find it.

Reflect & Write: You have already identified several relationships where the dynamic is parent-child. What actions can you take to move your position? And how do you imagine the other person would respond?

HANDLING CONFLICT

When you disagree with someone, what happens next? If you are afraid of conflict, perhaps you back down even before they know you have a different point of view. If you are too comfortable with conflict, perhaps you charge straight in and end up in an argument that damages your relationship. In this section you'll learn to notice that different perspectives are inevitable and become more comfortable in engaging in constructive conflict which values the insights that everyone brings. The following quote from Dudley Field Malone sets the spirit that we'll take with us over the next few pages: *'I have never in my life learned anything from any man who agreed with me.'*

My Relationship to Conflict

I hear many people say, 'I don't like conflict'.

Reflect & Write: Do you? When there is conflict or the early signs that a conflict may be brewing, what do you do?

When we're uncomfortable with conflict, we tend to employ one of five strategies:

1. Compromise (a bit of your idea, and a bit of mine)
2. Fake blindness (there is no conflict)
3. Ignore it (just move on)
4. Defer it (get someone else to decide)
5. Fight it out (attempt to win the debate)

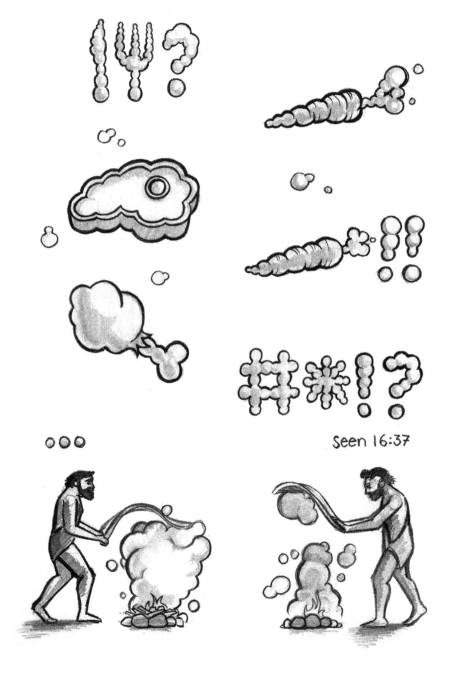

Seen 16:37

Reflect & Write: Consider each of the strategies in turn and attempt to find an example from your past when you have employed each of them.

Perhaps you found it easy to come up with examples of some strategies and they might be your 'conflict default state'. The second one on the list above is interesting. A large minority will say 'I don't have conflict in my life.' But I don't believe this is true. It's typically due to differences in how we categorize the word 'conflict'.

'Conflict' includes two armies fighting across a border; political parties fighting an election; Pepsi vs Coke; creationism vs evolution; and many more. In most of these cases, there is evidence of conflict because of 'clear-to-see' actions.

Have you ever had conflicting thoughts with yourself? 'I should go to the gym; not today though.' To other people, there is no obvious sign of this conflict – it's one of internal thought.

Have you ever negotiated with someone else about where you will go for dinner? Or what to watch on Netflix?

When we consider the word 'conflict', our definition is: 'two or more people have different thoughts about something'.

With this refined definition of the word 'conflict', can you accept that it's everywhere, every day and that at times you are blind to it? Even with the people that you love the most, you have different perspectives to them.

Reflect & Write: Considering a very good friend, or your partner – what subjects do you have different opinions about?

With these people, you simply accept that you have different points of view, without feeling forced to accept their point of view as being correct, (although secretly you'd love them to one day say 'you were right all along'!).

What if they don't really listen to your point of view? What if, when you are making your case they're clearly not listening, just waiting for you to pause for breath so that they can restate their case? What if you never get the space to make your point at all? It may not happen with your trusted friend, but it happens with some people in your network.

Reflect & Write: How does it feel not to be listened to?

Some people seem naturally able to stand tall in conflict, happily articulating their perspective in-depth, and revelling in it (they step into it). Others always shy away from it, go quiet, and disengage from the conversation (they step back from it).

Reflect & Write: Who do you know that sits at either end of the spectrum, and where do you sit?

Seeing the Whole
I say 'up', you say 'down'. I say 'black' you say 'white'. I say 'left' you say 'right'. 'Girl'. 'Boy'. 'In'. 'Out'. 'Day'. 'Night'.

When something exists, so does its opposite, and in many instances, a whole range of options between the two. Whatever point of view you hold, a contrary one exists. To understand anything fully we have to acknowledge and then appreciate the other perspectives. Yet to us, sometimes one perspective is so clear that we instantly discount the others. We become blinkered and dismissive, sometimes becoming even more entrenched in our way of seeing if our perspective is challenged.

Look at this picture, what do you see?

It's not a trick question. You see a square, with two dotted sides, and two solid sides. If we now imagine that this is 3D, we see a box with two dotted sides and two solid sides. How about in the picture below? What does the pirate see?

'I see a dotted box, agghh,' says the Pirate.

'Really, Mr Pirate, the box is clearly solid,' responds Lady Prim of Hampton Court.

'Well, shiver me timbers, Lady Prim, I believe that this time you are not correct. The box is quite clearly dotted.'

'My goodness, Mr Pirate, perhaps the time has arrived for that good eye of yours to be checked. The box is most certainly solid.'

'Oh no, it ain't. It's dashed, and my parrot 'ere agrees with me.'

'It's solid. Now come along, stop being silly, I have things to do.'

'IT AIN'T SOLID, AND I AIN'T GOING NOWHERE WITH THE LIKES OF YOU!'

'Well, there's no need to shout; there is nothing wrong with my hearing, just as there is nothing wrong with my eyes. And if you refuse to come with me, then I shall go alone. Goodbye, Mr Pirate.'

'GOOD RIDDANCE TO YOU, LADY PRIM.'

The origin of all conflict; two people seeing the same thing differently.

In this case, the Pirate wants to fight it out, while Lady Prim is OK to walk away, leaving the conflict unresolved. In this case, as in most cases, the argument ends with each person even more convinced they are right, and even less willing to listen to alternative suggestions.

At the start, Lady Prim and Mr Pirate probably didn't care much about this box – and at the end, they still don't care about it, but are consumed with negative thoughts about the other person. If the objective of the conversation was to establish the true composition of the box, it has been well and truly lost because of their lack of ability to enter the conflict positively; from the adult space.

Have you ever found yourself defending a position that you didn't know you had before a conversation began? In fact, have you ever found yourself passionately arguing for a point of view that you actually don't believe in, just because you don't want to back down?! Sure, you have!

Back to our box. If our pirate beckoned all his shipmates forward to stand right alongside him, what do they see? A dotted box! Have these other perspectives helped us to establish the composition of the box? No. Yet they would be in wonderful agreement because they see things the same way.

What if Lady Prim was off taking afternoon tea with Lord Prim, and couldn't offer her different perspective? All 20 pirates see a dotted box, and therefore it must be dotted. You see the danger of working with teams who all see things the same way.

To see the whole picture, we must seek to work with people who have different perspectives – in corporate-speak, this is termed 'diversity'. The word is often combined with the word 'inclusion', which means enabling all the voices to be heard.

Even the quiet ones. Especially the quiet ones! When we have diversity, and we have inclusion, then conflict is inevitable – different perspectives will be brought into the open, and the team will get a full picture of a situation. In a group situation, if there is diversity, and there is no conflict, what is going on?

It's because there is a parent-child dynamic. Some people feel inferior, belittled, undervalued, disrespected and therefore don't speak up. They are in the child position. If this is the case in your group – how do you maintain an adult space and enable others to move from parent to adult so that all the voices can be heard?

Giving People a Voice

Reflect on a group of people you spend time with. This could be your team at work, or a project group at Uni, or even a group of mates. It's likely that within the group, some people speak their mind readily – and you know their point of view on most things that come up. What about the quietest person in the group? They may outwardly appear to agree with the rest of the group, but they haven't shaped the direction of the conversation. When there is lots of boisterous chatter, it's easy for individual voices to be lost. The group loses a valuable perspective and the individual feels worthless.

Reflect & Write: Who is in this position, and what can you do to help them have their voice heard? If it is you, what can you do to bring your perspectives to the table?

We All See the World Differently

In the example above it's clear that the pirate and Lady Prim see things differently because they're standing in different positions, and therefore the visual sensory information received is different. However, even if the pirate and Lady Prim stood side by side, their five senses receiving the same inputs, they would have different internal representations of what they see. How does this work?

In our brains, the reticular activating system (RAS) connects the brain stem to the cerebral cortex through various neural paths. If our consciousness were flooded with all the sensory information available to it then it would be overwhelmed and unable to make any decisions. So the RAS filters and prioritizes information coming from the external world, controlling what appears in the mind's eye at any point of time. These filters depend on your life experiences, and therefore, everyone has a unique set of them, and this is why people have a different internal representation of what they experience in the outside world.

Remember this image? The sensory information being received by the guy in the top picture and the woman in the lower one is the same, yet their RAS filters are different. What they see in their mind's eye isn't a true representation of what's in front of them. The mind is working more like a projector than a camera. What the guy sees is a friendly social situation with lots of interesting people to meet. The woman sees a threatening situation with lots of opportunities to feel uncomfortable.

How you see things is guaranteed to be different from how someone else sees them. Sometimes these differences are obvious; sometimes subtler. You can't possibly see what another person sees, yet we assume we can because we're looking at the same thing. The only possible way to understand a different perspective is to ask the question: how do you see things? And then to listen with a truly open mind.

Jumping to Conclusions

Stephen Covey said, '*We judge ourselves by our intentions and others by their behaviour.*' But what else can we use to judge someone on? We can only judge what we see; we're not mind-readers. But for ourselves, even if the specific action we take came out a little different than we'd hoped it would, we can console ourselves that at least our intentions were good.

The observable action comes as a consequence of thought processes that we often cut short. From time to time, we jump to conclusions. Some people do this often, others less frequently. But we all do it.

Reflect & Write: Think of the last time you jumped to a conclusion about something that later turned out to be wrong.

Organizational psychologist Chris Argyris developed a model called the 'Ladder of Inference',[70] (first published by Peter Senge[71]) which helps to explain, and then correct what's going on.

Starting at the bottom of the ladder, we receive sensory inputs through our five senses, which pass through the RAS filters to give us a selective reality. We add meaning in order to interpret reality through our cultural lens and apply our existing assumptions. Based on these, we draw conclusions, from which we form beliefs, and take actions that seem 'right' because they are aligned with our beliefs.

Wow, you see how far it is from facts to actions! When someone behaves in a certain way and you can't understand why, it is because the nature of the rungs on your ladder are different to theirs. The sequence is the same, but the outputs are different.

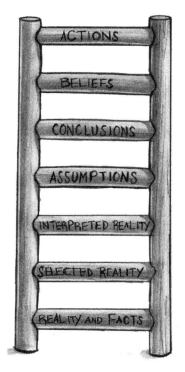

When you jump to a conclusion, it's because the rungs are working super-fast in your subconscious. The key to success is to slow down and allow your conscious mind to ask questions at each step. This is also the key to understanding someone else's behaviour. Remember, they believe that they are doing the right thing because it is aligned with their beliefs – so challenging them at this level can be perceived to be an attack on their belief system, causing a dramatic and disproportionate response.

You may have used the phrase 'they are making a mountain out of a molehill' because you think you are talking about a minor action, but they interpret it as an attack on their beliefs.

If your conclusions are different to someone else's, carefully descend the ladder with them until you can get back to reality and the facts that you can both agree on, and then climb the ladder together comparing notes about what you both now see as you climb.

Reflect & Write: Think of three situations where someone acted in a certain way, and you couldn't understand the logic of their behaviour. Who was it? What was the situation? What did they do? And how can you climb the ladder with them so that you can understand the belief on which it is based?

Good Conflict

It's only when two people use the 'fight it out' strategy that a difference of opinions becomes a heated argument. The opposing points of the two sides are out in the open, but nobody is listening and learning. With all the other strategies that are employed to avoid conflict at least one of the points of view goes unheard. So, what is the right strategy?

Step 1 – Seek to Understand

Henry Ford shares the thought: '*If there's any one secret to success, it lies in the ability to get the other person's point of view.*' When we say, 'get it', we mean really get it. This means noticing how our ladder of inference is working as they are talking. What assumptions are we making? What filters are working to distort the reality of their words? We don't want our interpretation of their reality, what Ford is talking about is the ability to stand in their shoes to experience their reality.

Here's an important point. By listening and enquiring you do not necessarily agree with their point of view, you are simply expanding your awareness of the viewpoints that can be held.

Aristotle said, '*An educated mind can entertain a thought without accepting it.*' The language you use with the other person makes it clear that you are exploring their reality by using the word 'you' or 'yours' a lot. 'How do *you* see things?' 'What conclusions are *you* drawing?' 'What assumptions underpin *your* conclusions?' 'What facts support *your* thinking?'.

The test is that you can explain their argument back to them with detail and clarity that is surprising. Allow them to make tweaks to your words until they are completely satisfied that they have been fully heard and understood.

In the first step, you make the other person feel great – they are being respected, honoured and valued. But there are some typical traps that can catch you out even at this stage:

Defensiveness: Can you really listen when you feel as though you need to defend yourself from an attack?
Inner Voice: Your inner voice will be chattering away, and therefore preventing you from giving them your full attention.
Time: Your internal clock will be ticking. If you only have 10 minutes for this topic, and you spend all of it exploring the other person's argument, then where does that leave you? Therefore you leap ahead, make assumptions, and jump to conclusions.

You will notice that you are in control of all the things that could derail this first step.

Step 2 – Invite an Invitation to Share

Make it clear that you have another perspective (notice the non-confrontational choice of words: it's simply a different way of seeing things), and then ensure you fully do step 1. Keep asking the questions, keep being inquisitive until you really can explain the other position better than they can. When the conversation starts, you could use words like: 'We see things differently. I would love to explore your perspective so I can really get where you're coming from, and only then, give you some space to ask me a bunch of questions that help me to articulate my thoughts to you. If this means that we need to find some more time to continue the conversation, would you be open to that?'

The groundwork is laid. There is a subtle moral contract in place: I will listen to you, and then you will listen to me.

The only thing that derails this step is if you skip it or do it too late. You need to set the agenda, so that it's clear for both of you. If you don't then a) the other person may not know you have an alternative point of view to share, and b)

they will think that spending so much time on their opinion means it's the only one that matters.

Step 3 – Share the Full Ladder

Help the other person to see what you see. Remember that they have different filters, so their RAS produces a different 'selected reality' to yours. Talk through your assumptions, allow your interpreted reality to be tested. The goal isn't to get them to change their mind but to help them to see what it is that you see so that they can explain it back to you.

What will derail you here is that the other person probably hasn't read this book. They will be flipping from parent to child – interrupting, not listening, and generally hijacking the agenda to reiterate their view of the world. It's an ingrained habit, so give them a break and continue to hold the adult space: 'Thanks for the interruption, and for reiterating the importance of this specific point to you / for adding a new thought. Let me check I still fully understand your point of view, and then let's return to you helping me to articulate my thoughts to you.'

Be patient. It may take a few rounds of holding the adult

space for them to realize that the old games that have worked for years are no longer being played.

At this point most conflicts melt away. The misunderstanding, the misinterpretation, the misalignment, the lack of respect that causes the vast majority of conflict (or the avoidance of conflict), is gone. In the tiny minority of cases, a decision needs to be taken and it's a clear choice between going one way or another. The conflict ends when a decision is taken, based on all the available facts, a full awareness of all the different perspectives. It may go your way, it may not, but you and everyone else will feel as though their contribution was valued.

Summary

When there is more than one person, there is more than one perspective on anything and everything. If the perspectives are not aired, you're missing an essential ingredient that has helped homo sapiens to evolve. Having the ability to embrace conflicting points of view, to explore them with an open mind and an open heart is a wonderful skill to aspire to and develop. Perhaps you don't have a great relationship with conflict – yet.

Reflect & Write: What will it take for you to develop a more adult relationship with the concept of conflict? To embrace the value of conflict, what will you begin to do?

DEALING WITH UNACCEPTABLE BEHAVIOUR

At some time in your life you've said 'I can't believe they just did that', and you've thought it on many occasions. What did you do about it? What should you do about it? What will you do about it?

Reflect & Write: When have you witnessed, or been on the receiving end of unacceptable behaviour? What is unacceptable behaviour?

Do those people accept that their behaviour is unacceptable? What are the possible answers to this question?

1. They do it with full awareness that their behaviour is unacceptable and yet are unrepentant.
2. They know they are acting inappropriately and feel guilty inside.
3. They are aware of their actions but do not categorize it as 'unacceptable'.
4. They lack self-awareness that their actions are considered by others to be 'unacceptable'.

Reflect & Write: Test the above assumptions to see if they do cover all your experiences of unacceptable behaviour. Consider four specific instances when someone has acted unacceptably. Who was it? What did they do? Which of the above categories does it fall into (1–4)?

I CAN'T BELIEVE THEY JUST DID THAT ! THAT IS **NOT** OKAY!!

When these things happen, you have two options:

1. Rise above it, let it go and manage your own internal state so that you're not negatively affected by it (Chapter 3).
2. Give feedback.

Principles of Feedback

It may be natural to judge the person, categorising them as 'bad', but it's important to separate the person from the action. It's a person's behaviour, rather than their personality, that should be the subject of the feedback. Principle number one, therefore, is to be very specific about the behaviour that you feel is unacceptable.

Who is doing the judging? That's you! Not society, or 'everyone', or 'a few of us'. You must take ownership of your judgement rather than hiding it. And remember that your judgement comes through your life filters – your subjective reality, your assumptions, and your beliefs about what is right and what is wrong. The feedback is more about you than it is about 'them'.

Nobody can control you, and you can't control another person. You can give the gift of feedback in a perfectly empathetic way, but whether it is well received or not cannot be your responsibility. They can choose to change, or they can choose not to. That's their prerogative.

A Model for Feedback

There are several different models for giving feedback, most with acronyms that spell something memorable – and all of them pretty much saying the same thing.

> **Observation:** Explain, with simple clarity, the specific action you have observed.
> **Feeling:** Describe how you personally felt as a result of this action.
> **The Ask:** Suggest different actions that could be taken next time and be open to exploring options.

You can see how this model removes any judgement about

the other person and instead helps them to understand the impact on you. This method works for any of the four categories of unacceptable behaviour because it is conducted from the 'adult' space, and therefore shouldn't trigger the parent or child in the other person.

Reflect & Write: Return to your list of people who have behaved unacceptably. Using the feedback model, consider how you could structure your feedback to them.

Practising Feedback

Now you know the theory let's set some homework so that you begin to build the muscle. With everything that we introduce in the book it's better to start small and develop your technique before unleashing it in full. So letting go of any thoughts of anybody that would require deep reserves of courage to address, consider a couple of people with whom you have a good foundation of trust.

Reflect & Write: What specific behaviour would you like to address that would help to deepen your relationship with them?

Twice as Nice

Remember 1, 4, 9 from page 67? It's easy to focus on the 15's – the things that are not good – but I bet these people do at least twice as many things that make you feel good as make you feel bad. The feedback model works for these too. Not only does giving positive feedback make the other person feel good, but it is also likely to stimulate them to keep repeating the behaviour more often, and therefore you get to feel great more of the time.

'Thanks for all your help,' is nice to hear. But, by running your feedback through the feedback model first, the impact is doubled. 'Last week, when you saw me getting stressed about everything on my to-do list, you offered me help and took a specific task off my list. I felt a real sense of relief and could sleep better again. If you see me struggle again, I will welcome you asking if I've got too much on my plate.'

Many times, people simply don't know the positive impact that they have on you. So begin to tell them, and watch the smiles grow.

Reflect & Write: Name two people that you'd like to give positive feedback to, and plan what you want to say using the feedback model.

TRUST
When you are in a trusting relationship, oxytocin hormones flow around your brain and you feel safe enough to take risks and expose your vulnerabilities. When there is mistrust your amygdala triggers the fight-or-flight response, adrenaline and cortisol are released, and you feel afraid or angry. The level of trust that exists defines the quality of your relationships, so what is it, how does it develop, and how do you recover it when it is gone?

Let's first get your thoughts out on paper with a series of reflect and write questions:

Reflect & Write: What causes you to trust people? Consider people from both your personal and professional life.

Reflect & Write: When you think of a person that you trust wholeheartedly, how does it feel, and as a result, how do you behave around them?

Reflect & Write: How readily do you place your trust in people? Are you over-trusting, trusting all the people all the time and regularly feeling let down? Or, are you tight-fisted with it saying, 'They have to earn my trust'? Place an 'x' on the axis:

OVER-TRUSTING   MISTRUSTING

Reflect & Write: How about you, are you a trustworthy person? What makes you trustworthy?

Reflect & Write: Who don't you trust, and specifically, why don't you? Think of three people you don't trust, why not?

Reflect & Write: Notice how it feels to think about how these people betrayed your trust. How you behave around them is affected by your feelings – when there is mistrust, how do you act?

Your Betrayal

Just now you wrote down the reasons why you are trustworthy. However, research by Charles Feltman[72] found that *we generally judge others to be less trustworthy than ourselves*', which means that 'it is very likely that some of the people in your life judge you to be less trustworthy than you consider yourself to be'.

Reflect & Write: How may others consider you to be less than wholly trustworthy? What do you sometimes do to betray the trust that others have in you?

Big gulp! That was slightly sickening to write down. We all want to consider ourselves to be trustworthy, yet some of our actions get in the way. The boot is on the other foot, it's not just other people that betray my trust, I also betray theirs. You are not perfect, and neither are they.

Trust Deconstructed

What is 'trust'? You wrote down a long list of what causes you to trust people, and we use the word 'trust' to summarize the whole list. We then judge a person's character as trustworthy or not. But the basket of attributes that build up the picture of trust is just too jumbled to make sense of. In his wonderfully simple book, *The Thin Book of Trust*,[73] Charles Feltman deconstructs the word 'trust' into four distinct categories. Summarized, they are:

1. **Sincere:** you are honest; you say what you mean and mean what you say.
2. **Reliable:** you meet your commitments and keep your promises.
3. **Competent:** you have the necessary ability to do things well.

4. **Caring:** you are considerate towards others.

We can now notice how difficult it can be to score full marks across all four 'distinctions'. Let's take the last one, it may be the most important on the list for you and is perhaps the most important one of all. Because you want to really care for other people, do you:

- Find it difficult to say 'no', and therefore overload yourself and fail to meet some of your commitments?
- Really try to please people by accepting to do things that you don't have the expertise to do well?
- Shy away from being honest about how you feel for fear of hurting their feelings?

It may be easy for you to be 100 per cent trustworthy in how you care for people, but at what cost? If you're praising something small ('great, you found the lamp shade') while there's an elephant in the room that you are not addressing, then how much trust is there really?

You may be considered untrustworthy because of a perception of a lack of sincerity, reliability, or competence. Which feels harsh and unfair, but it's exactly how you judge others. The word 'trust' is just too broad to be helpful when we're scrutinising the nature of our relationships – so we're going to use the Feltman distinctions to help move things forward.

You 'Deconstructed'

Earlier you wrote a list of the things that made you trustworthy, and then a second list of the things that made you untrustworthy. These lists may help you with the following assessment.

Reflect & Write: Taking Feltman's four distinctions, write them in order from strongest to weakest. My list would be reliable, competent, sincere, caring. What's your order?

Reflect & Write: What comes last on your list, and how does this affect people's ability to trust you?

Reflect & Write: Because we have a growth mindset, we can say 'I am not great at this thing... yet.' It will take practice and perseverance to get better, so how will you start?

People Deconstructed

You have relative strengths and weaknesses across the four distinctions, and so do others. Instead of labelling other people as untrustworthy, let's examine what we have observed (not what we have imagined) about others and therefore have a go at ranking their relative strengths and weaknesses.

Reflect & Write: Consider five people who you don't entirely trust. Arrange the list of distinctions from their strongest to their weakest.

Is there a pattern forming? Does the same distinction keep appearing near the end of the list? If so, then you may have an unusually high degree of sensitivity towards betrayal in one dimension. Are you fair, or is your bar of expectation set unreasonably high? Perhaps or perhaps not. By getting into the details, do your feelings towards these people change?

Because I don't always show great compassion for others, I could be labelled as untrustworthy by you, and this label would affect how you behaved around me. With a greater level of insight, you may now say, 'I can completely trust Todd to deliver what he said he would, and with great quality too, however, he sometimes steamrollers in and doesn't listen to other people. I don't feel as though he values or cares about what I have to say.'

Todd is no longer a wholly bad guy (phew!), but he does have some traits that are difficult to accept. Which takes us back around the loop, to page 254, and how to deal with unacceptable behaviours. What is your next move? Live with it, or address it with feedback?

The Trust Quality Standard

The International Organization for Standardization develops a set of globally understood and agreed-upon methods for assessing quality. They don't, however, produce international standards for anything like 'how to measure Trust'. Which means that every individual is free to set their own standards, and then measure others based on their own definition of quality.

Which is a problem! Because my standards are different from yours. And I sometimes allow myself to bend my own rules:

'I will always ensure my meetings end on time as a sign of respect for the commitments that people have following the session, except if it feels like we're ending on a negative tone, then it's OK to carry on.'

'I will be honest and speak my mind, except if I'm afraid of some negative consequences.'

Not only do you not know my standards but you can also make poor assumptions about my standards based on evidence of my behaviour. But at least there are some generally accepted standards for essential things like timekeeping.

Richard Lewis blogs about how different cultures understand time:

'Time is money, and therefore we shouldn't waste a drop of it', says the New Yorker. 'The sun rises and sets, the moon waxes and wanes, we are born, and we die, and we return in another form – time is endless', says the Tibetan. While the 'Spaniards, Italians and Arabs will ignore the passing of time if it means that conversations will be left unfinished.'[74]

Your cultural upbringing establishes your inner relationship with time. Even with something so measurable and standardized, there is no universal agreement on what constitutes 'good timekeeping'. So there is also no black and white around it – 'lateness' turns out to be subjective based on internal beliefs rather than the position of the hands on a clockface.

Based on your experiences, you've developed a set of assumptions that underpin good and bad behaviour. You then measure others based on your imagination of the 'perfect human', and when someone doesn't measure up to your model of perfection. Boom! They have let you down and are untrustworthy!

Let's backtrack and use the ladder of inference on page 248 to help us. We're making assumptions – based on what? Our interpreted reality – the one that we have imagined. So, we step down a couple of rungs. What facts or evidence is there that I can make an assumption about a person? In the beginning when you first meet someone, you have very little evidence, so your assumptions should be broad and easily changed. As you begin to get to know someone more, the assumptions can be refined and updated. When they do something you had assumed they wouldn't, then instead of being outraged or surprised, you can simply use the new evidence to update your set of assumptions about them. Nobody is letting you down; they're simply revealing an aspect of themselves that had previously been hidden from you.[75]

Deepening Trust

If there is no mistrust in a relationship then we have the opportunity to consciously grow the level of trust that exists. With some individuals you feel an instant rapport, share surprisingly openly and feel a deep connection with them in almost no time. With other acquaintances, you've maintained a professional separation – you don't really know them, and they don't really know you.

Back in Chapter 1, on page 13, we introduced the Johari windows. The level of trust between two people is equal to the combined size of their 'open' boxes. Back on page

14, you made a list of the things that are in your 'hidden' box; that you choose to keep private. To deepen trust, you slowly and gently begin to reveal parts of yourself, and gently and patiently give the other person the space to share what they feel comfortable to share.

It should be a reciprocal thing and should be allowed to move at a natural pace, but do notice if it has begun to stall or stagnate. If there is no longer any new revealing going on, then you can expect the level of trust between you to flatline – and this may be OK for some relationships.

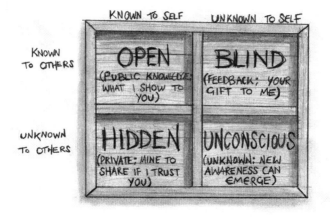

When you share something with someone that reveals something new about you, then you open the door for them to do the same. Not necessary in the next sentence, or even during the same conversation, but sometime in the future. There's no need to force it, nor suggest that you should do all the revealing while they keep you at arm's length. Trust is a dance that needs both partners to be dancing to the same rhythm, but sometimes someone has to take the lead.

Asking about someone else is, of course, a great way to take the lead. It's often avoided because of a fear of prying (definition: 'inquiring too closely into a person's private affairs'). You will have things that you don't want other people to ask you about, and everyone has these things – so yes, don't pry. When we 'pry a door open', we use a sharp tool and brute strength to force our way through it, however, when you enquire about a person there are loads and loads of doors that are simply waiting to be opened and need zero force. In fact, a great many of them are like automatic doors: you simply walk close to them, and they throw themselves wide open. So yes, don't get the tools out and pry, but don't shy away from all the doors.

Non-prying, inquisitive questions that encourage people to reveal more about themselves in a comfortable disclosure kind of way include:

- Where did you grow up, do you have any brothers or sisters, and what are they like?
- What's the origin of your surname, first name, middle name?

You can take the lead by asking these types of questions in a first meeting, and if you don't know the answer already, you can ask them of people you already know. You can also take the lead by choosing to share something that is currently hidden. It's hard to plan these things in detail, because then you'll be rehearsing what you want to say, and that will prevent you from coming across as natural and authentic. So instead of deciding what, let's just decide who.

Reflect & Write: Who would you like to deepen your trust with, and are ready to expand your 'open' box when the situation naturally arises?

What To Do When You've Broken Trust

From time to time you break the trust that someone has in you, and it's usually completely unintentional. But remember, we are being judged by our actions and not by our intentions. Furthermore, our actions are being judged against a set of standards that we can't be exactly sure about. So it can feel profoundly unfair. Nevertheless, you're aware that someone has lost trust in you, and that hurts. So what should you do about it?

According to Feltman, '*the only known antidote for the betrayal of someone's trust is to acknowledge it and apologize for it.*'

Remember you have not suddenly become a wholly untrustworthy person, so find out precisely which of the four 'distinctions' you are perceived (their perception is their reality) to have violated. Then what specifically did you do (or not do)? You are *not* apologising for being you but how your behaviour has impacted their ability to trust (and therefore feel safe) around you.

Limit the excuse-making; but if the situation has the potential to occur again, be open about it and jointly work through what a better course of action would be. For example: 'Last week I gave you a report that missed some key figures and caused you to be unable to answer key questions from the director. I am really sorry for not delivering a full report to you, and for causing you some reputational damage in front of other people. I am also concerned that it may happen again – I rely on getting data from the UK office and haven't found an effective way to influence them. What could I do so that you aren't in the same situation again?'

It may be time for you to eat some humble pie.

Reflect & Write: Who doesn't fully trust you, what has caused that loss of trust, and how can you now rectify it?

Trust can develop over time, and you can enhance the speed of it by consciously enhancing behaviour across all four distinctions – both in yourself, and using feedback, in others. Remember that your behaviours are driven by your beliefs, but they are being judged through the filters of someone else's life experience. Remove the intense emotion caused by language like 'betrayal of trust', and instead seek to tweak specific behaviours, and be respectful of others' rights to see the world differently.

HOW TO BE INTERESTING

Some people seem adept at entering new groups, striking up a conversation, and connecting well with people. This may not be you, and you'd be in the majority. Say the word 'networking' and the shivers of apprehension start. The art of conversation is an essential life skill yet not one we're taught at school. With a few simple techniques, anyone can be interesting; here we'll learn how.

Reflect & Write: Who do you know that is a good conversationalist, and why do they deserve this accolade?

Reflect & Write: What about you? It may be situation-dependent, so reflecting on your recent experiences, when were you a good conversationalist, and when were you not? What made the difference?

It's pleasing to remember the times when you were a good conversationalist. You probably felt relaxed in the company of the other people, that there was mutual respect and a balanced reciprocal nature to listening and talking. When it goes badly, it can feel excruciating, unequal, one-sided, and leaves you feeling under-appreciated or concerned that you came across as a bore.

Reflect & Write: Now, consider the people in your life that are poor conversationalists. What traits do they have in common?

There are a couple of traits that come out most often:

1. They talk too much and don't listen.
2. They are detached and seem disinterested.

To be interesting, simply practise doing the opposite all the time: listen with genuine attention.

Entering new groups

Think of the last time that you entered a new group. This could be a class at school or college, a new place of work, a team meeting with new colleagues, dinner with the girlfriend's parents or an assessment centre. How did you feel just before entering the room, and what was causing that feeling?

It is the same for almost everyone because we all have the same desire for acceptance. It's hardwired into the animal instincts of all primates because if we're rejected by our clan when we're very young, we die. Our behaviours are driven by a fear of rejection, and so as far as possible, we try to conform so that we 'fit in'.

In a new group, there is no foundation for trust, so individuals are reluctant to be vulnerable. They keep the idiosyncrasies that make them genuinely individual under wraps, and instead we engage in 'small talk' about super-safe topics like the weather, rather than the juicy and potentially controversial topic like global warming.

If you feel anxious when joining a group, feel OK about this – it's normal. It's our animal brain keeping us safe from rejection. What happens next is the key. For some people, animal fear overrides natural human instincts to be social, and they create an impenetrable protective bubble around them. The bubble takes different forms – when nervous, some people talk and talk, while others are totally consumed by the internal chatter and are therefore outwardly silent.

Smile – First Impressions Count

This takes us back to Chapters 3 and 4: how to overcome your fears and manage your state. If you find entering groups is overwhelming, then return to those chapters and work through the techniques to access a resourceful state of mind.

Your body language is talking loudly whether you are speaking or not – giving off signals of being welcoming and warm, or cold and hostile. Remember that trust is the foundation block of any relationship and how you enter a room gives signals of how caring and sincere you are. In this regard, nothing works as powerfully as a simple smile aimed in the direction of each and every person present. They feel acknowledged by you, you begin to make one-on-one connections with the fleeting eye contact that comes with it, and something else happens too – the smiles spread!

So even if your heart is pounding, and the inner voice is chattering – find a way to give a nod and a smile.

Nothing to Say

I once heard a story about an experiment conducted many years ago to test a theory that the most interesting people were those that were interested in others. The organizers of a networking event invited 30 people to an evening of drinks and canapés and afterwards asked the participants to write down the names of three people they found most interesting and would like to be connected with for a follow-up conversation.

Five of the individuals were instructed beforehand to reveal nothing about themselves, to anyone, all evening.

If asked something, they deflected the question by asking one of their own back to the other person.

When the surveys were collated, and the requests tallied up – who do you think were judged to be the most interesting people in the room?

The five people who had said nothing about themselves!

Carnegie[76] concludes: '*You can make more friends in two months by becoming interested in other people than you can in two years by trying to get other people interested in you*'. He continues,[77] '*nothing is as flattering to another person as getting your exclusive attention*', and this is brought to life by third Carnegie quote:[78] '*Mum, I know that you love me very much because whenever I want to talk to you, you stop whatever you are doing and listen to me.*'

Is Everyone Interesting?

If you assume that only some people are interesting then you're unlikely to truly follow through with the advice from the last section. Will you turn the conversation over to another person and simply ask questions if you believe that they are boring? No!

What I have found is this. When people don't feel safe they stick to small talk, and this gets very boring very quickly. However, when great trust exists and they feel free to allow their inner thoughts to come tumbling out without fear of judgement – wow, EVERYONE has a story to tell, opinions to share, and passions to get excited about.

When you start with the assumption that everyone is interesting, you can allow your natural curiosity to get to work. If the other person isn't interesting, it's because you haven't laid the foundation for the trust that is necessary for them to open up to you. So enter the dance of trust, be vulnerable yourself, and as you share some of your stories, they feel more open to sharing some of theirs.

Reflect & Write: Who have you written off as 'boring'? Can you allow yourself to believe that there is an interesting side to them that you haven't seen yet?

From Small Talk to Deep Stuff

Where are you from? Did you have a long journey? Have you worked here long? What course are you studying? What do you do? Start with any of these questions, get a one-line answer, then a return question: 'how about you?', give a one-line answer. Dialogue over. Uncomfortable silence. Next question from the list. Sound familiar?

To get things really flowing, the secret is to ask a second more inquisitive question before you take your turn to respond to the first one. The second question digs a little deeper, and you get some insight into the real person. You have met plenty of accountants, but behind the job title every one of them is unique, so go looking for the person behind the mask.

Instead of having a bank of one-line questions, develop a set of questions that flow nicely from one to another. Here are some examples:

Backstory questions:

- Where are you from? Have you always lived there? Where did you grow up? Is that where your family is from?
- What is your name? How do you spell it? Am I saying it right? Does it have any meaning? What's your surname? Do you know any history of your family name? What about a middle name? Where

does that come from?

- Do you have any siblings? What are they like? Are you close? What are they doing now?
- Are you more like your mum or your dad? What do they do? What are they like?
- What do you do? What did you do before that? How did you get into it? What do you like most about it? Is your team nice? How about your boss?
- What's the best holiday you went on as a kid? What's the best job you ever had? What's the best memory you have from growing up? What's the best thing that happened to you?
- What do you like to do in your free time?

Dreamy questions:

- If you could do any job, what would it be? If you didn't have to earn money, what would you do? When you were young, what was your fantasy job?
- If you could go anywhere in the world, where would you go? What would be your ideal holiday?
- What is your perfect Friday night? If you chose a famous person to hang out with, who would it be, and what would you do?
- If you could order any food as your last dinner, what would you choose?
- If you could learn anything, what would it be? If you had the time and the money, what hobby would you most like to take up?

You can see how all the questions start with something very safe and 'normal', and how they increase their depth over time. Please remember, though, this isn't an interrogation –

conversations are reciprocal. You are allowed to share your responses to the questions too, it builds the trust necessary to get to the next level of depth.

When reading through the list of example questions, there are some that you would like to be asked, and some that you would find more challenging to answer. So be natural, go with the ones that make you feel comfortable – your comfort will come out in your body language and your tone and therefore make the other person feel more at ease.

Reflect & Write: Perhaps selecting from the list above, perhaps writing your own: next time you meet someone for the first time, what line of questions would you feel comfortable with?

Conclusions

How to be interesting sounds like some dark art, and we're either born with a 'gift of the gab', or we're not. This isn't true – to be interesting, simply follow these five principles:

- Accept that the fear of rejection is a natural human condition when entering a group.
- Use the techniques from Chapters 3 and 4 to manage your state sufficiently so that you can access a smile.
- Assume that everyone is wonderfully interesting once they feel comfortable enough to talk freely.
- Practise asking questions in a series that get increasingly deeper.
- Show appreciation by being curious and bringing your undivided attention.

LISTENING

Whatever the topic, in this chapter, we have repeatedly underscored the importance of listening. Whether it's to deepen friendships, overcome conflict or be perceived as interesting, listening is the key, and it's not as straightforward as you perhaps imagined!

You may hear someone talking – that's the sound waves entering your ears but listening requires your concentration too. You're only 'listening' when your brain is processing what it hears and makes meaning from the words and sentences (and the body language that accompanies them).

Behaviours of Listeners

I was at a party a few months ago, the drinks had been flowing and while waiting to get served at the bar I was watching a group of four people chatting on the edge of the dancefloor. Because that was what they were all doing. All of them chatting, at the same time, to one another. All four mouths were moving non-stop, and it was pretty clear, even from a distance, that nobody was listening.

You have all experienced this at some time in your life, so let's not dwell on the obvious examples of bad listening, but instead notice the behaviours of the good listeners.

Reflect & Write: When you think of the good listeners in your life, what do they do well?

Reflect & Write: Sometimes, you will also be a good listener, and at other times you don't listen so well. When you are not a good listener, what are you doing badly?

Bad listening

You have noticed that you sometimes listen badly. Can you recognize some of these bad traits in yourself?

Distracted

You may not entirely ignore someone if they are talking directly with you, one-to-one. But you're ready to be distracted – by anything. Many years ago, when mobile phones were a novelty, I was having a chat with a colleague whose mobile phone rang. He answered it and proceeded to have a conversation with the caller while I stood like a lemon in front of him. Nowadays I have friends who think it is OK to pick up their phone and begin to browse through it while I am talking to them. Do you know people who do this? Does your attention sometimes get pulled away from a conversation? Your behaviours make it clear that you are ignoring the other person.

Wandering

Have you ever been in a conversation with someone, and over time, as they continue to talk, your mind wanders? Has it ever wandered so far away that you completely forget that the person is talking to you? You catch yourself and come back to the conversation with a jolt desperately trying to slip right back in again as though you've never been away. For the entire time the person is talking you've been on autopilot, and they know it because you've been saying 'uh-huh', and 'yeah', and 'uh-huh', and 'yeah', and 'uh-huh' and 'yeah', and when you come back from your mind wander you break the monotony by throwing in an 'exactly', or 'definitely', before returning to 'uh-huh', and 'yeah', and 'uh-huh', and 'yeah'.

Biased

Your mind is wandering, but you're also listening out for trigger words or phrases which will cause your full attention to come back to the talker. This is often the case when we're in conflict with the other person. While the other person is talking, we take the opportunity to give the brain time to construct our own next awesome point, while also keeping half an ear on their chatter in case something that they say would be useful in our argument. In biased listening, you hear only the parts of the conversation that interest you.

Hijacking

You listen and hear all the words, and you relate to them by comparing what you hear with your life experiences. When the other person pauses, or when you interrupt them you take over (aka hijacking the conversation), based on your own frame of reference. You are likely to:

1. **Evaluate:** Agree or disagree with what is said.
2. **Probe:** Ask questions to satisfy our own needs.
3. **Advise:** Hand out unsolicited opinions on what should be done.
4. **Interpret:** Make meaning of what they are saying from your own point of view.

Most people listen with the intent to *reply*, not to *understand*. At any given moment, they're either speaking or preparing to speak. Next time you're in a conversation, notice where your attention is!

Good Listening

Thankfully, *7 Habits of Highly Effective People* author Stephen Covey[79] described a deeper level of listening, which he called 'empathetic listening'. He describes it as 'getting inside another person's frame of reference.'[80]

In this mode of listening the habits of judgement and preconceptions are silenced, and you've gone beyond being open-minded (where you're accepting that different world views exist). You're now in the realm of listening with an open heart. When you can do this, you connect with the other person not just on an intellectual basis, but on an emotional one too.

Remember the ladder of inference from page 248? If you're in bad listening mode, then you're inferring a lot about the other person. When you're employing Empathetic Listening, you're able to see each rung of the other person's ladder. They'll say, 'wow, you really get me!'. Now imagine if you 'get' everyone you work with, and everyone you live with, and everyone you hang out with. It doesn't mean you agree with them; it simply means that you know (not guess or assume) where they are coming from. And it feels great!

Reflect & Write: Who really 'gets' you? And how does it feel?

Being a Better listener

We all have moments when we listen poorly, and even though we've now read some theory about it, we'll do it again. So instead of making a 'new promise' to ourselves never to do it, let's set an intention to create some conditions where we're less likely to fall into it unconsciously.

As a first step in the right direction, stop whatever you are doing, put your phone away, turn your body to face the talker directly, and give them your full attention, or agree a time when you can. Don't multitask and listen. Just this evening, I was writing this section of the book, and my daughter burst into the room full of excitement to tell me about a funny YouTube video she'd just watched. My head was fully in writing the book and I didn't want to lose my flow, so I turned to her and said, 'I'd love to hear all about it, and listen to you properly, give me 15 minutes, and I'll come to your room.' And 15 minutes later she got my full, undivided attention.

Reflect & Write: Who do you often give half of your attention to, and what is it that typically distracts you? Choose five people who sometimes receive poor listening from you and make an intention to remove the distraction and give them undivided attention.

To overcome biased listening, you need to develop a technique to help you to hear everything a person says rather than just those things that pass through your RAS filter. Have a go at summarising back what you have just heard. Use your own words but attempt to avoid adding your interpretation. Your goal is for the other person to say, 'yes, that's exactly what I was trying to say'.

A reminder, you are not agreeing with them or giving their argument greater weight, you're simply acknowledging that you understand where they are coming from. You may like to begin your summary with the words, 'Let me check that I fully understand your point of view and correct me if I don't get things exactly right, I'd really like to see how you see things.'

Reflect & Write: Whose ideas or thoughts do you dismiss without fully exploring their point of view?

At this level, there is a balance to be struck. Sometimes it is good to be active in a conversation – your probing and interpretation bring real depth of understanding. It's helpful. The question is about where your balance is. Can you stop yourself from doing it? Can you really bite your tongue and prevent yourself from hijacking the conversation and making it about yourself? Or perhaps you have the exact opposite challenge, maybe you lack the courage to bring your point of view into a conversation and are therefore hiding your contribution from others. Where do you sit on the scale?

TOO LITTLE
CONTRIBUTION

TOO MUCH
HIJACKING

Reflect & Write: In what situations should you be more mindful of your hijacking tendency, and what do you now intend to do differently? Or, when are you missing the opportunity to contribute?

Listen Like the Buddha

If you can imagine the Buddha sitting and listening to you talk, you begin to imagine what Empathetic Listening looks

like in practice. I would like you to bring more 'open-hearted', Buddha-like listening to your relationships.

Reflect & Write: Who will you bring an open heart to more often, and therefore listen to fully and completely with no desire to hijack?

Concluding Thoughts

The quality of your relationships largely determines the quality of your life. Water those that bring you most emotional satisfaction by deepening the way you listen with an open heart. Treat conflict as a requirement for seeing the world afresh and give well thought through feedback if you are hurt by others. Readdress imbalance in relationships by seeking to hold the adult position, and dive into the four dimensions of trust to build positive relationships.

Above all, use the techniques from this book to manage your internal state, crack a smile at every opportunity, and honour the presence of other people by being fully present with them.

CHAPTER 9
EMOTIONAL INTELLIGENCE

IQ is Nothing Without EQ

We've all experienced times when our emotions have got in the way of our thinking, but we might not realize they are also the **key** to thinking. We literally can't make decisions without making use of emotion.[81]

How smartly we use our emotions is measured by our emotional intelligence (EQ), and includes:

- How well we know and accept ourselves for who we truly are.
- The ability to be aware of and manage our emotional state.
- Having empathy to develop positive relationships.
- Being grounded in the realities of life, while having aspirations for the future.

Most people first heard the term 'emotional intelligence' around 1995 with the publication of Daniel Goleman's best-selling book, *Emotional Intelligence, Why it Can Matter More Than IQ*. He laid out the case that EQ is the best predictor for life success. No matter how you wish to define success!

Non-profit organisation Six Seconds examined 75,000 individuals across 126 countries[82], and not only concluded that success and EQ are linked, but also that, '*EQ has twice the power of IQ to predict someone's performance*'.[83]

Because 'success' can mean different things to different people, Six Seconds cleverly used an average of four broad and balanced variables (effectiveness, relationships, wellbeing, and quality of life) to come to an 'average success' score. They agree with Goleman – EQ really is the best predictor of life success.

The extent to which you have emotional intelligence is broadly related to your upbringing, but thankfully this doesn't mean that your success is pre-determined, because unlike IQ, which is generally accepted to be fixed after the teenage years, emotional intelligence can be developed throughout life. And the best thing? You've been developing it since the first page of this book.

Emotional Intelligence isn't another new topic that we're covering here in Chapter 9. Instead, it is simply the perfect way to pull together the strands of everything you have already done and give it a single, simple, powerful label.

HOW MUCH DO I HAVE?

There is no global standardized test for EQ, and you will find many different versions available online – some of which are free. But you've already taken a test that is highly likely to correlate with any online EQ assessment that you can take. It is right back at the start of the book on page 2.

Update your responses now by re-rating your answers to the following statements on a scale from:

| strongly disagree | disagree | neutral | agree | strongly agree |

- I know and accept myself for who I am.
- I believe that I can become good at anything that I choose to put my mind to.
- I maintain a positive emotional state of mind regardless of what is going on around me.
- I push through fear to accomplish things that are uncomfortable.
- What I do is aligned to a deeply held sense of purpose.
- I make the most of life by using my time wisely.
- I am like a battery, always full of energy and ready to go.
- I enjoy trusting, respectful relationships with everyone in my life.

To get a crude metric that you can track over time, use the following scoring system. For every statement where you responded with Strongly Agree score 12.5, Agree = 10, Neutral = 5, Disagree = 2, and Strongly Disagree = 0. Add up the total points to get your Own Life percentage.

Remember, that EQ is developable. Wherever your scores are now they can shift upwards provided you believe they can, and you are prepared to put in the (sometimes uncomfortable) effort.

GROWING EQ
The self-assessment above gives you some insight into your relative strengths and weaknesses relating to emotional intelligence, but it doesn't enhance it. Enhancing it requires action. If you noticed your scores are higher than when you

started the book, it's likely because you have experimented with some new actions. If you have got this far and haven't seen a shift in EQ, it's because you now have cognitive intelligence (you've read about what makes a difference) without the corresponding experiential lessons that are required to shift your life.

You've already covered everything you need to enhance your EQ. The question is, to what depth did you choose to take it? I've been working in emotional intelligence for about a decade, and I constantly find that I have new things to work on to improve myself. Writing this book has led to another layer of questions, and therefore another layer of insights about myself.

Nobody has perfect EQ. Therefore, development in this area is never 'done'. Having said that, it's not a subject that requires endless research. All the topics that you need to cover are included in this one short book. The key isn't to make it an academic subject, read once and set aside, but a practical one. Whatever the specific topic, the learning cycle is simple:

1. Reflect on where you are now.
2. Imagine where you'd like to be in the future.
3. Determine an action that will take you forwards.
4. Have the courage to undertake the action.
5. Reflect on the outcome of the action
6. Back to step number 1, and repeat, repeat, repeat.

Reflect & Write: Taking a look at your scores on the self-assessment. Which two statements would you most like to put under the spotlight of development over the next six months? Flicking back through this book, which sections feel most relevant to your development goals? What is your intended next action?

You can go around the cycle multiple times and get more and more value from the topics and reflection questions in this book. You can come back to the Own Life self-assessment each time and rescore yourself – noticing how you see yourself change as the years go by.

Right now, put a date in the calendar. When will you come back to the book for a second, third, fourth time?

CHAPTER 10
CONFIDENCE AND SELF-BELIEF

Look at the following statements:

- Self-belief is confidence in your own abilities, worth or judgment.
- Self-respect is pride and confidence in yourself.
- Self-regard is a consideration for yourself.
- Self-confidence is a feeling of trust in your abilities, qualities and judgement.

They all mean broadly the same thing, and whichever one you choose, it is the essence of everything. Do you trust yourself?

If you do, then you believe that you can achieve your goals and you'll find evidence that you're right, and the fortitude to persevere. If you don't trust yourself, then you will find evidence to back up your limiting self-judgement, and step back from challenges. I love this Henry Ford quote: 'if you believe in yourself, then you can succeed. If you don't, then you can't'.

You have felt this throughout the book. Whenever you

have been set a challenge, you naturally had a belief about it – either you could do it, or you couldn't. This determined whether you would try to do it, or you wouldn't. Or perhaps it's not quite so black and white.

Perhaps you said to yourself, 'You know what, I don't know if I can do it, so I'm going to give it my very best shot. Then I'll learn from that shot, readjust my aim and give it another go. And another. And another.' This is the belief that you can learn to do practically anything – this is the growth mindset.

If self-belief is the essence of everything, how do you get more of it? Let's find out.

When Are You Confident?

Score yourself 0 – 10 on how confident you are.

Did you find yourself having the following inner conversation, 'It depends on the circumstances'?

Of course, it does. So, scoring 'you' as a whole person isn't very helpful. With some people, you feel completely at ease. With other people, their mere presence is unsettling, and you begin to doubt yourself. Confidence depends on who is in the room with you. There are also likely to be occasions when you feel very confident, for example when you do something routine at work, and occasions when you feel less confident, perhaps when you've been asked to present in front of a group.

It's easy to notice the low confidence moments because the body can set off all the fight or flight symptoms – a racing pulse, scrambled thoughts, sweaty palms, shallow breathing, lightheadedness etc.

Reflect & Write: Acknowledge 10 situations that cause you to feel low confidence.

This may have been an easy task for you to complete. Your low confidence moments may come with 'full-on' body experiences, and each moment may be pre-lived with anxiety before the event, and then re-lived over and over afterwards. The amount of time your mind spends in these situations is likely to be much longer than the actual situation itself. Is this true for you?

Reflect & Write: OK. Let's go searching for the opposite scenario. Can you find 10 moments when you felt high in confidence?

Is that more difficult to pin down? It's because we don't notice these moments; there is no heightened state within the body to help us notice them. Most of the time we just get on with something because we've learnt how to do it well, and we're on autopilot. While we're doing these things, our minds actually might be living in the negative fantasy world of a forthcoming low-confidence moment.

When I feel competent at what I'm doing my mind wanders – I don't focus on how good I am at doing what I am doing. I make awesome pizzas from scratch and simply love the whole process from dough-making to serving up. I've made them so often that I can do it without thinking. I don't dance around the kitchen high-fiving and singing 'everything is awesome', I just get on with it.

Spend a little more time on the list of high confidence moments. You're not necessarily looking for a physical 'high', simply things that come easy and take no mental or emotional energy.

What would happen if you only ever faced situations that you felt supremely confident in? You'd be living the same life over and over again, week after week. Never growing.

This may be attractive to some people. But not for you. You want more than that.

Let's reframe things a little.

Those low confidence moments that you listed are not defined by your level of confidence. They are retitled as – 'the things I am yet to master'. As your skill level develops, quite naturally, so does your confidence. There's no dark magic at play here. Look back to all the definitions at the start of this chapter. They are all about how much you trust your own ability. To build self-confidence is simply to build your capability to face the situations that you are likely to face in life.

Read this next line: 'I'm not a confident person.' That's the last time that you're going to say this to yourself. I'm not asking you to blindly lie to yourself and now say, 'I'm a supremely confident person.' I am asking you to take the whole person (you) out of the judgement, and phrase it with a growth mindset by saying, 'There are situations I face when I feel lower in confidence because I haven't mastered them yet.'

Which leads us nicely to two questions. What are those situations, and how can you master them?

Reflect & Write: Imagine that it is possible. Imagine that you really could master some of those situations where you currently feel low in confidence. Which ones would they be? Pick 3–5.

JOURNEY TO MASTERY

There are four stages to developing competence, and everything you have just listed sits in the lower-left quadrant of the chart below. You are aware that you lack the skill. Whatever skill you have mastered, you were once here. Then you took lessons, or received guidance, or learnt from failure until you became proficient (conscious competence). Then you practised and practised, and over time, it became easy (unconscious competence).

The first step to mastery and therefore greater confidence is to become just slightly more skilful at dealing with the situation. Then just slightly more skilful, and on and on.

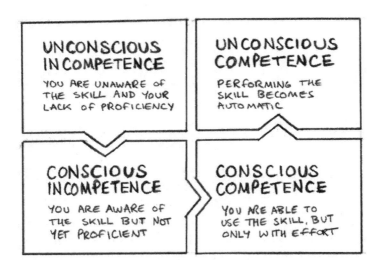

Reflect & Write: How can you become more skilful? Taking the situations that you would love to master, what first step could you take to develop your skill?

Now things are starting to move. Believe that you can make this small first step, and then take it.

When I try to imagine that I can one day master something that I'm currently incompetent at (like speaking French), it can feel like an impossible dream. It can feel daunting. Yet one small step leads to another, and the daunting limits simply dissolve as I approach them.

You don't need to know how you will take the final step,

the answer to that will emerge when you take the one before it. All you need to do is start walking.

Self-belief

If you spend most of your time being asked to do something that you do not have the capability for, you will naturally have low confidence. But is it really most of your time, or just a small amount of time that your mind exaggerates?

Are you really incompetent, or simply not perfect? Who are you judging yourself against? My pizzas are good (for an amateur), but if I measure myself against a *MasterChef* champion, I may conclude that I lack skills.

If your internal narrative is 'I am no good at stuff', then your RAS (reticular activating system, see page 247) gets to work to make sure that all the evidence that backs this up is passed to your consciousness and all the evidence to the contrary is deleted. It's a self-fulfilling prophecy. Which is why we're changing the narrative so that your RAS can get to work on allowing self-serving messages through its filter (rather than the self-defeating ones).

The narrative changes from this day forward. From 'I am no good at...' to 'I will get better at... by doing...'

Sure, while your human brain is being all logical and saying, 'yes we can,' the chimp brain is saying, 'watch out you might look stupid'. Because that's its job.

The only way to Own Life is to step into moments of difficulty and realize that you can handle it. Each time you do this, you realise you can handle more and more. Henry Ford said: '*Whether you think you can or think you can't, you're right*', so now it's over to you.

Time to step in and do the first actions you listed above. The first step takes courage, and it is a wonderful journey from here to self-belief.

CLOSING THOUGHTS

Who am I, and where am I heading? Who are you, and where are you heading? I hope one day our paths intersect, and when they do, you come to say hi.

If you'd like to do that right now, head to www.ownlife.me to connect with me and your fellow Own Life readers as we continue our life journeys together.

My hope is that I have been able to guide your journey. My wish is that you feel OK with simply being you. Not just some of you; all of you. My wish is that you realize that happiness and success and love all come from within. My wish is that you let your light shine so that you brighten up the world. My wish is that as you do so, you will light the fire in hearts of everyone around you. My wish is that we come to value what's deep inside every human being: compassion, love, creativity, ambition, courage, sacrifice.

I would like you to know that you are already more amazing than you are giving yourself credit for. It's time for you to throw off the shackles of social conditioning, tame the chimp, believe in yourself, and really live this life. Now go Own Life!

ACKNOWLEDGEMENTS

When I was 20 years old, I bought a book on 'how to write a book'. I had in my mind an autobiographical account of life and what I made of it as I lived it. While I took a further 20+ years to mature sufficiently to actually write it, my school years clearly shaped the trajectory of life. Thanks first to all the teachers at Upton Priory Infant School, and then for 11 years at Kings School in Macclesfield, particularly those that gave their free time to allow me to play sports pretty much non-stop. My school years, though, are defined by the enduring friendships that I am lucky enough to have. To Rick, Rick, Andy, Johny, Tim and DB – you shaped me.

The naïve Birmingham graduate grew up in the corporate world at Rolls-Royce and Britvic Soft Drinks – thanks to everyone I worked with and for, you allowed me to make mistakes. You gave me your trust. Thank you.

The leap into self-employment is described by many as brave, but I was filled with courage by small drops of encouragement from a huge cast of characters with whom I networked in my first year 'alone'. To everyone that: met for coffee; chatted at events; invited me into their circle; introduced me to friends; listened to my dreams; gave feedback on my plans; recommended a book; or opened doors... Your contribution may feel small, but your impact is significant. Please keep giving in the selfless way that you did for me.

To Nigel and Jefferson. My teachers, mentors and friends. A large number of the words that fill this book, I first heard coming from your mouths. Thank you for LeadNow. Through it, over the years, I honed the flow, tested theories, tweaked the questions, trialled models. Without LeadNow, this book wouldn't exist. Without the two of you, I wouldn't be me.

To write well, I need to feel on top form. I need the rest of my working life to be in good order – no distracting dramas. Nothing could have been better for my writing than spending the bulk of my non-writing days working on projects with the Quest team: Esther, Svend, David, Steffi, Martina, Katrien, Dani, Floris, Hana, Jan, Natalia, Rebecca, Axel. Your humour, energy, spirit, goodwill, insight, and empathy are infectious. The work we did together, outstanding.

My clients and workshop participants. I think of you as I write. What questions have you asked, what challenges have you faced? Which models served you, which activities unlocked something, which book recommendation landed well. How you reacted to our conversations has shaped the content and tone of this book. It's written for you, and your friends and colleagues.

El Davo. Words came out of my head and onto a screen. You were then the very first person to read them. You read them, interpreted them, tried them out for yourself, and this meant that you really got them before trying to develop an illustration to depict them. Our monthly ideation sessions have been a wonderfully enjoyable fixture in my calendar for a very long time; I've never felt so creative or imaginative than when I'm with you. The illustrations are out of this world. You bring the book to life, you make it flickable, you make me smile with the humour you put into them. I am very, very lucky to be working on this with you.

In fact, I'm lucky to have had a wonderful team during this entire project – thank-you editor Sandy, designer Catherine, proof-reader Jackie, and indexer Marie. You've helped this first-time author produce something he's proud of.

If 95 per cent of our personality is determined by the time we are seven years old, then my parents can justifiably take the majority of the credit for this book. Thanks for instilling a strong work ethic, a strong sense of self-belief, and for role-modelling 'thinking of others before yourself'. The older I get, the more I realize that the simple way you live your life is the 'right' way.

For Olive and Wilbur. If you are the only two people ever to read this book, I would be a happy dad. I love you. x

Finally, to Tam. Without you, I would be a brain without a heart, using my intellectual ability to succeed professionally in life, but at what cost? In 1996 you opened my heart, and from that moment on, everything was different. Your unwavering support, which allows me to follow my dreams, is unreal. The way you treat people, with unnecessary kindness and thoughtfulness is continually eye-opening and heart-warming. I hope one day that I too will have the same selfless attitude that you do. You're awesome. Thank you for everything, always.

NOTES & REFERENCES

1 Eagleman, D. (2016) *The Brain, The Story of You*. Edinburgh: Canongate Books. Page 6

2 Warner, J (2012) *Coaching Models: Johari Window*. Blog. readytomanage.com. 20 March 2012.

3 First heard from Nigel Linacre (NigelLinacre.com)

4 Metaphor conceived by Jefferson Cann (JeffersonCann.com)

5 Opfer, C. (2014) *'Does your body really replace itself every seven years?'* 6 June 2014. HowStuffWorks.com. <https://science.howstuffworks.com/life/cellular-microscopic/does-body-really-replace-seven-years.htm>

6 Radford, B. (2011) *Does the Human Body Really Replace Itself Every 7 Years*. 4 April 2011. LiveScience.com. <https://www.livescience.com/33179-does-human-body-replace-cells-seven-years.html>

7 Maslow, A. (1997) *Motivation and Personality*. Pearson.

8 Duhigg, C. (2013) *The Power of Habit*. London: Random House Books.

9 Duhigg, C. (2013) The Power of Habit. London: Random House Books.

10 Duhigg, C. (2013) *The Power of Habit*. London: Random House Books. Page 283.

11 Baumeister, R & Tierney, J. (2012) Willpower. London: Penguin Books. Page 1.

12 Baumeister, R & Tierney, J. (2012) *Willpower*. London: Penguin Books. Page 50.

13 Dweck, C. (2012) *Mindset*. London: Robinson.

14 Ericsson, K., Krampe, R., and Tesch-Romer, C. (1993) *The Role of Deliberate Practice in the Acquisition of Expert Performance*. Psychological Review, vol. 100. No3, 363-406

15 Gladwell, M. (2009) *Outliers: The Story of Success*. London: Penguin.

16 Kashdan, T. and Biswas-Diener, R. (2015) *The Upside of Your Darkside*. New York: Plume.

17 Peters, S. (2012) *The Chimp Paradox*. London: Vermilion. Page 69.

18 Photo credit: Phil Noble, PA Archives, Press Association Images

19 Neill, M. (2014) *Why aren't we Awesomer*. TED 2014. <https://www.youtube.com/watch?v=xr6VawX2nr4>

20 The 149 Effect is the brainchild of Steve Head, I heard him deliver the principle of it during a humourous and inspiring keynote talk to the AGCAS conference in 2017. To see videos of Steve in action, or book him for a keynote of your own, go to www.stevehead.co.uk

21 Peters, S. (2012) *The Chimp Paradox*. London: Vermilion. Page 70.

22 Gawdat, M. (2017) Channel 4 News, 9th April 2017 <https://www.channel4.com/news/google-exec-seeks-the-equation-for-happiness>

23 Gen Kelsang Nyema, TEDx Greenville 2014. <https://www.youtube.com/watch?v=xnLoToJVQH4&vl=en>

24 Jeffers, S. (2007) Feel the Fear and do it Anyway. London: Vermillion.

25 Layton, J. *How Fear Works*. 13 September 2005. HowStuffWorks.com. <https://science.howstuffworks.com/life/inside-the-mind/emotions/fear.htm>

26 Jeffers, S. (2007) *Feel the Fear and do it Anyway*. London: Vermillion. Page 12

27 Jeffers, S. (2007) *Feel the Fear and do it Anyway*. London: Vermillion. Page 68

28 Robbins, M. (2017) *The 5 Second Rule*. USA: Savio Republic.

29 Robbins, M. (2018) *The five elements of the 5 second rule*. <https://melrobbins.com/blog/five-elements-5-second-rule/>

30 Mind. The Mental Health Charity <https://www.mind.org.uk/information-support/types-of-mental-health-problems/anxiety-and-panic-attacks/anxiety-treatments/#.W-rk2WacY_U>

31 Mind. The Mental Health Charity <https://www.mind.org.uk/information-support/types-of-mental-health-problems/anxiety-and-panic-attacks/panic-attacks/#.W-wQ5macY_U>

32 Practical exercise developed by Jefferson Cann (JeffersonCann.com)

33 Duckwork, A. (2013) *Grit: The power of passion and perseverance*. TED April 2013. <https://www.ted.com/talks/angela_lee_duckworth_grit_the_power_of_passion_and_perseverance?language=en>

34 Wilson, C. (2017) *Exact: A Coaching Approach to Goal Setting*. Culture at Work http://www.coachingcultureatwork.com/wp-content/uploads/2018/04/Coaching-for-

Performance-EXACT-a-Coaching-Approach-to-Goal-Setting.
pdf, and for greater depth on EXACT goal setting: Wilson,
C. (2014) "Performance Coaching: A Complete Guide to
Best Practice Coaching and Training". London, Kogan Page

35 Covey, S. (1989) *The 7 Habits of Highly Effective People.*
London: Simon & Schuster. Page 98.

36 Whitmore, J. (2002) *Coaching for Performance: Growing
People, Performance, and Purpose.* Nicholas Brealey
Publishing, 3rd edition.

37 Gallwey, T. (2001) *The Inner Game of Work.* USA: Random
House.

38 The metaphor of the bus with inner voices depicted as
characters was first conceived by Floris Verbeij

39 Curtin, C. (2006) Fact or Fiction?: *NASA Spent Millions to
Develop a Pen that Would Write in Space, whereas the
Soviet Cosmonauts Used a Pencil.* ScientificAmerica.com.
<https://www.scientificamerican.com/article/fact-or-fiction-
nasa-spen/>

40 Ries, E. (2011) *The Lean Startup.* London: Portfolio Penguin.

41 Urban, T. (2014) *Your life in weeks.* Wait But Why. 7 May
2014. https://waitbutwhy.com/2014/05/life-weeks.html

42 Unknown. Origin of the story is unknown; this version is from
DevelopGoodHabits.com <https://www.developgoodhabits.
com/rock-pebbles-sand/>

43 Vrabie, A. (2014) *How to improve your time management
skills with the urgent-important matrix.* Sandglaz Blog
Archive. <http://blog.sandglaz.com/the-urgent-important-
matrix/>

44 Clear, J. Procrastination: *A Scientific Guide on How to Stop
Procrastinating.* JamesClear.com. <https://jamesclear.com/
procrastination>

45 Jeffers, S. (2007) *Feel the Fear and do it Anyway.* London:
Vermillion.

46 Covey, S. (1989) *The 7 Habits of Highly Effective People.*
London: Simon & Schuster

47 Loehr, J & Schwartz, T. (2003) *The Power of Full
Engagement.* New York: The Free Press.

48 Covey, S. (1989) *The 7 Habits of Highly Effective People.*
London: Simon & Schuster. Page 287

49 Salzgeber, N. (2017) *Why Working in Sprints Maximizes
Human Productivity.* Medium.com. 13th February 2017.
<https://medium.com/@nilssalzgeber/why-working-in-

sprints-maximizes-human-productivity-e8f2eba3d98b>
50 Loehr, J & Schwartz, T. (2003) *The Power of Full Engagement*. New York: The Free Press.
51 Ally. (2018) *Inflight passenger announcements*. AirOdyssey. net. 25 November 2018. < https://airodyssey.net/reference/inflight/>
52 Much of the following section is indebted to the research conducted by Mathew Walker and published in his book 'Why we Sleep'. London: Penguin.
53 Loehr, J & Schwartz, T. (2003) *The Power of Full Engagement*. New York: The Free Press.
54 Walker, M. (2018) *Why we Sleep*. London: Penguin.
55 Mitchell, H., Hamilton, T. Steggerda, F & Bean, H (1945). *The chemical composition of the adult human body and its bearing on the biochemistry of growth*. Journal of Biological Chemistry 158, 625-637. <http://www.jbc.org/content/158/3/625.citation>
56 Cook, K. (2018) *37% of people in the UK never exercise or play sport*. Kantar UK Insights.<https://uk.kantar.com/business/health/2018/37-of-people-in-the-uk-never-exercise-or-play-sport/>
57 Ekkekakis, P., Hall, E.E., Van Landuyt, L.M. & Petruzzello, S. (2000). *Walking in (affective) circles: Can short walks enhance affect?* Journal of Behavioral Medicine, 23 (3), 245–275
58 Alfermann, D. & Stoll, O. (2000). *Effects of Physical Exercise on Self-Concept and Wellbeing*. International Journal of Sport Psychology, 31, 47–65
59 Salmon, P. (2001). *Effects of Physical Activity on Anxiety, Depression, and Sensitivity to Stress: A Unifying Theory*. Clinical Psychology Review, 21 (1), 33–61.
60 Zschucke, E., Gaudlitz, K. & Strohle, A. (2013). *Exercise and Physical Activity in Mental Disorders: Clinical and Experimental Evidence*. J Prev Med Public Health, 46 (1), 512–521.
61 Kahneman, D. (2012) *Thinking Fast and Slow*. London: Penguin.
62 Gifford, J. (2018) *The secret of the 10% most productive people? Breaking!* DeskTime. 14 May 2018. <https://desktime.com/blog/17-52-ratio-most-productive-people>
63 Kahneman, D. (2012) *Thinking Fast and Slow*. London: Penguin.
64 Frankl, V. (2004) *Man's Search for Meaning*. London: Rider.

65 Wikipedia contributors. (2019, April 2). Maslow's hierarchy of needs. *In Wikipedia, The Free Encyclopedia.* Retrieved 15:24, April 2, 2019, from <https://en.wikipedia.org/w/index.php?title=Maslow%27s_hierarchy_of_needs&oldid=890614393>

66 Carnegie, D. (2006) *How to Win Friends and Influence People.* London: Vermilion. Page 19

67 Boutin C. (2006) *Snap judgments decide a face's character, psychologist finds.* Princeton.edu. 22 August 2006. https://www.princeton.edu/news/2006/08/22/snap-judgments-decide-faces-character-psychologist-finds

68 If you would like to know a little more about Transaction Analysis, check out the summary here: <http://www.ericberne.com/transactional-analysis/>

69 Berne, E. (2010) *The Games People Play.* London: Penguin Books.

70 Argyris, C. (1990) *Overcoming Organizational Defences: Facilitating Organizational Learning.* New Jersey: Pearson Education.

71 Senge, P. (1990) *The Fifth Discipline.* Michigan: Doubleday/Currency.

72 Feltman, C. (2009) *The Thin Book of Trust.* Bend: Thin Book Publishing. Page 6.

73 Feltman, C. (2009) *The Thin Book of Trust.* Bend: Thin Book Publishing.

74 Lewis, R. (2014) *How Different Cultures Understand Time.* BusinessInsider.com. 01 June 2014. <https://www.businessinsider.com/how-different-cultures-understand-time-2014-5?r=US&IR=T>

75 Thanks to Jefferson Cann for this terminology

76 Carnegie, D. (2006) *How to Win Friends and Influence People.* London: Vermilion. Page 56

77 Carnegie, D. (2006) *How to Win Friends and Influence People.* London: Vermilion. Page 96

78 Carnegie, D. (2006) *How to Win Friends and Influence People.* London: Vermilion. Page 91

79 Covey, S. (1989) *The 7 Habits of Highly Effective People.* London: Simon & Schuster. Page 236 to 260.

80 Covey, S. (1989) *The 7 Habits of Highly Effective People.* London: Simon & Schuster. Page 240.

81 *In Descartes Error,* neurologist Antonio Damsio describes that patients with brain damage in their emotional centers

are unable to weigh choices and evaluate options. Emotion, it seems, tells people what is reasonable, credible, and desirable. Harper, 1995.

82 Miller, M. *Emotional Intelligence and Success.* 6seconds. org. <https://www.6seconds.org/2019/03/12/white-paper-emotional-intelligence-and-success/>

83 Miller, M. *Emotional Intelligence and Success.* 6seconds. org. https://www.6seconds.org/2019/03/12/white-paper-emotional-intelligence-and-success/

INDEX

ABOUT THE AUTHOR

Todd Eden's sole mission in life is to bring out the best in people. It wasn't always this way! Right through childhood and through his first couple of careers, he was insatiably competitive – great at bringing out his personal best and achieving results, but not always with great consideration for everyone around him.

Thankfully he married someone who simply oozes kindness. The resulting upgrade, Todd version 2.0, retains his authentic ambition to win at life but now defines winning as 'bringing out the best in others'.

This mission has taken him around the world working with multi-national companies; into the lecture theatres of a third of the UK's universities; and deep into the lives of his personal coaching clients.

He remains a passionate student of self-development and has been living and breathing it daily for decades. At live events he enjoys bringing his unique combination of profound life shifting moments with belly laugh humour to thousands of people. It's his wish that this book brings out the best in many thousands more.

Connect with Todd at www.OwnLife.me

ABOUT THE ILLUSTRATOR

From a young age, El Davo enjoyed art, and from seeing other people's reactions, he learned he had a talent. He attributes some of this to being curious and observational of his surroundings - or a daydreamer as others might put it. Those around him saw the need to nurture this talent well before he was aware of it himself.

He was lucky enough that his older sister was an artist, always there to offer invaluable support and encouragement when he was growing up. She lived in London at the time and regularly took him around the city to different galleries, as well as showing him all the graffiti and street art hotspots. Later she convinced him to pursue an art education beyond sixth form and attend art college, and after that, university.

Initially, he never felt like he'd earned this talent, but nonetheless felt obliged to make the most of it. He constantly strives to improve, for both the buzz of exceeding his own expectations and the joy it brings others. He especially loves to hear of people inspired enough to get back into doing art themselves. He firmly believes there's a huge pool of untapped creative talent in society, stuck inside people who haven't had the support and encouragement he's been fortunate enough to receive.

Connect with El Davo at www.eldavo.co.uk or on Instagram @eldavooo

Printed in Poland
by Amazon Fulfillment
Poland Sp. z o.o., Wrocław